Bali Rai

(un)arranged marriage

**Annotations by
Mechthild Hesse**

Ernst Klett Sprachen
Stuttgart

Herausgegeben von Prof. Dr. Mechthild Hesse, Freiburg

1. Auflage 1 ⁷ ⁶ ⁵ | 2012 11 10

Alle Drucke dieser Auflage sind unverändert und können im Unterricht nebeneinander verwendet werden. Die letzte Zahl bezeichnet das Jahr dieses Druckes.
copyright © Bali Rai 2001
first published by Random House Children's Books
this edition copyright © Ernst Klett Sprachen GmbH, Rotebühlstr. 77, 70178 Stuttgart, 2007.

Internetadresse: www.klett.de / www.lektueren.com

Alle Rechte vorbehalten.
Das Werk und seine Teile sind urheberrechtlich geschützt. Jede Nutzung in anderen als den gesetzlich zugelassenen Fällen bedarf der vorherigen schriftlichen Einwilligung des Verlags. Hinweis zu § 52 a UrhG: Weder das Werk noch seine Teile dürfen ohne eine solche Einwilligung eingescannt und in ein Netzwerk eingestellt werden. Dies gilt auch für Intranets von Schulen und sonstige Bildungseinrichtungen.

Fotomechanische oder andere Wiedergabeverfahren nur mit Genehmigung des Verlags.

Redaktion: Paul Newcomb
Umschlagfoto: Avenue Images GmbH (Stockdisc)
Fotos: Seite 4: Random House Children's Books; Seiten 180,181: Fotosearch RF (Digital Wisdom), Waukesha, WI

Sources of additional texts: Commission for Racial Equality; Office for National Statistics, UK
Druck und Bindung: GGP Media GmbH, Karl-Marx-Str. 24, 07381 Pößneck
Printed in Germany

ISBN 978-3-12-578040-8

About the Author.................................... 4

(un)arranged marriage.............................. 5
Additional texts 177
Immigration from India, Pakistan and Bangladesh........ 177
Statistics on the Ethnicity of Leicester and the UK 178

Maps
The Midlands in the UK................................ 180
The Punjab in India and Pakistan 182

Abbreviations used in annotations:
AE	American English
BE	British English
ca	circa
e.g.	exempli gratia; for example
etc	et cetera
inf	informal
sb	somebody
sth	something
vulg	vulgar

ABOUT THE AUTHOR

Bali Rai

Born in 1971, Bali Rai grew up in an ethnically rich part of Leicester and, apart from five years in London, has lived in Leicester all his life. He left school with eight GCSE's, and English was always his favourite subject. He did three A-levels at a local sixth form college – none of which was English Literature, which he now regrets. He went on to graduate from South Bank University in London where he earned a degree in politics. Before becoming a professional writer he held various jobs, from tele-salesman (selling goods over the telephone) to bartender. Although a full-time writer, he also visits many schools around the UK.

Bali Rai has been writing short stories and poetry since the age of eight. His writing is grounded in the reality that he has seen since he was a child. As the only member of his family to graduate from college, he uses his writing to encourage the people around him to read books, speaking to them in their own language about situations they can identify with.

Since publication in May 2001, **(un)arranged marriage**, his debut novel, has won many, many awards, as well as receiving national media coverage. His other works include **The Crew**, which was published in March 2003 and won the Leicester Book Award. Bali Rai has described it as "a thriller for teenagers set in the harsh reality of inner city life." **Rani & Sukh**, published in May 2004, is a gripping tale that crosses the generations with a tale of forbidden love. **The Whisper** appeared in May 2005 and, as a hard-hitting, sometimes violent tale of underground drug dealing and gangland crime, is the sequel to **The Crew**. **The Last Taboo** was published in June 2006. It is another hard-hitting novel, about two teenagers facing up to the consequences of racial prejudice between Asian and black communities. **The Angel Collector**, a crime mystery story, came out in 2007. Set in Britain, it tells of a teenager's nationwide search for his best friend. This tense and exciting story ends up in a remote farmhouse in Scotland that is home to a racist cult...

Bali Rai enjoys reading other children's authors like Roald Dahl and Sue Townsend. He loves music, especially reggae and in particular Bob Marley.

prologue

november 30th

The toilets in the motorway service station at Leicester Forest East stank of disinfectant. But at least they were warm compared to the biting cold wind that was kicking up outside in the car park – where my two brothers Harry and Ranjit were waiting for me. Waiting to take me to Derby, to a wedding – my wedding. A wedding that I hadn't asked for, that I didn't want, to a girl who I didn't know. They must have sat there waiting for me, laughing to themselves about how I had finally succumbed to their way of thinking, their way of life. A good Punjabi man at last, after years of being a tearaway, a rebel, a junkie and a philanderer. At least, that was what they had called me at various times.

I thought about my old man, waiting in the gurudwara in Derby, smiling a forced smile as the alcohol in his blood ate away at a little more of his liver, dreaming his once-technicolour dreams that were now played out in a sepia-tinted haze, dulled by the disgrace that was his youngest son. Me. Come to think of it his smile might actually have been genuine. After all, I was doing the right thing, at last. Restoring the pride and honour that I had destroyed with my wayward actions during the previous four years. I'm sure he must have been standing there, content in the knowledge that his beloved Punjabi culture had won out against the dirty, corruptive, white culture of the country which he had chosen to make his home. Like my brothers and the rest of my family, he chose to see only what he wanted to see, not what was really there, like some lovesick fool.

You see, if they had bothered to open their eyes they would have seen me: seventeen, angry, upset but determined. Determined to do my own thing, to choose my own path in life. They would have seen the marker left in those toilets at Leicester Forest East and realized that, underneath my ill-fitting suit, I had on my real clothes. That in my head was a hip hop tune that summed up

---

1 **Leicester** [ˈlestə] big city (ca 280,000 inhabitants) in the industrial East Midlands of England – 5 **Derby** [ˈdɑːbɪ] big city (ca 220,000 inhabitants) not far from Leicester – 8 **to succumb to** [səˈkʌm] to give way to superior force *(erliegen)* – 9 **Punjabi** [pʌnˈdʒɑːbiː] man from Punjab, province of eastern Pakistan – 10 **philanderer** a man who gets involved sexually with many different women – 12 **gurudwara** (Punjabi: doorway to the "Guru") a place of worship for the Sikhs, a religious group of India; also serves as a meeting place for initiation and wedding ceremonies – 14 **technicolour** a special process for making cinema films in colour (trademark) – 15 **sepia** [ˈsiːpiə] the reddish-brown colour of old photographs – 15 **tinted** lightly coloured – 15 **haze** state when the heat disturbs one's view of things in the distance *(Dunst)* – 16 **disgrace** shame – 16 **Come to think of it** Now that I think about it, … – 17 **genuine** real, authentic – 19 **wayward** [ˈweɪwəd] unruly, rebellious – 26 **to bother** *(here)* to care, to make an effort

exactly how I had them. They thought they were finally playing me, that I was dancing to their tune, when all the while I had them dancing to mine. It's kind of hard to explain the journey that I've made over the last few years, but I'll try because I believe that it's a story worth telling.

part one

four years earlier

Chapter One

'No way! I'm not getting married.'

I was shouting, something that I didn't do often. My oldest brother, Ranjit, had provoked it. I had come home from school and heard him and his wife having sex in their bedroom. I'd ignored them and gone into the kitchen to get myself a bowl of Frosties, but he had come downstairs, mumbling something about exercising, his moustached face all red from exertion. I know that I'd only just turned thirteen at the time but I wasn't a child. Like I didn't know what they were doing up there! It was just embarrassing, that's all. But then, after telling me a complete lie, he started banging on about how I would end up just like him.

'One day, Manjit, you'll be like me. Married to a nice Punjabi girl, thinking about babies.' It would have been all right if his wife, Jas, hadn't walked into the kitchen as he was saying all that stuff to me. They'd only been married for a few months and it was bad enough having to call her *phabbi-ji*, Punjabi for sister-in-law. Man, all she ever did was giggle. I just ignored them in the end, taking no notice of what Ranjit was saying. I tried not to take much notice of any of my family, full stop!

I hated being called Manjit too. Manny, that's what my name was. *Manny*. Not Manjit. That was a girl's name. There was this girl called Manjit in my class at school and all my friends teased me about it. Even my teachers called me Manny. If they wanted a reply. My brother *knew* how much I hated being called that so he made the most of it, the fat, smelly, hairy idiot. And as for being the youngest, well, that brought its own heap of grief too. Every joke seemed to be at my expense, as though one of the only reasons for my existence was to amuse my older brothers. There was Ranjit, who I've already mentioned, and his giggling wife, Jas – and then Bilhar who everyone called Harry. He was sixteen and already engaged to a girl who he had never met before. My parents had shown him a photo of a friend's daughter, caked in make-up and wearing a red sari, and he had said 'yes', just on the strength of that. But then again, that was the way things were in my family. Arranged marriages, preferably as soon as school was finished with.

---

7 **exertion** [ɪgˈzɜːʃən] hard work – 11 **to bang on** (*BE inf*) to continuously talk about sth in a boring way – 27 **heap of grief** much pain – 28 **at sb's expense** *auf Kosten von* – 34 **sari** [ˈsɑːriː] long piece of cloth that you wrap around your body, mostly worn by Indian women

I had two older sisters, too, both of whom were married with kids of their own. Dalbir, the eldest, was twenty-five and always seemed more like an aunt than a sister. The other one, Balbir, was twenty-one and had just had her first kid, a son. Balbir lived with her in-laws in Gravesend whilst Dalbir lived in Coventry with hers. That's the way it was in most Punjabi families; girls become members of the family they marry into and call their in-laws Mum and Dad. I had never really known either of my sisters because they were so much older than me. I was only six when Dalbir had got married, to an immigrant from India. He'd been working illegally for some uncle in a hosiery sweatshop. Marrying my sister gave him his right to stay in England. In Balbir's case, my old man had made an arrangement with a friend of his, almost like a business agreement, just so that Balbir's husband would be able to stay in England too. Man, the only thing missing was the financial aspect. It was all too weird for me, something I just couldn't understand. How could anyone marry a person they'd never met. How could that work? Not that I'd even ever had a girlfriend up to that point so I was no expert, but still, I just couldn't get to grips with the whole idea.

My parents were odd too. My old dear, my mum, well she was just like a stranger who never spoke to me unless she was asking what I wanted for dinner, or shouting at me for pissing about. She never asked me what I was feeling or what I was thinking or anything like that. At school I'd hear all my mates going on about how their mums had helped with their homework. Mine never even bothered to find out if I did any homework, never mind help me with it. Not that she could have anyway. I don't think that she ever went to school.

And my dad, well, he ran the family with fear. He was always either at work or sitting around, pissed on Teacher's whisky, shouting at everyone. He got angry all the time, maybe at something he'd seen on the TV or some problem at work, or sometimes for no reason at all. I'd never seen him hit my mum or anything like that. With her and my sister-in-law he just shouted a lot which scared them enough anyway. I had seen him hit my brothers though, whenever they were out of order, which was not that often because they were basically turning into newer versions of him and that was what he wanted all his sons to be.

---

11 **hosiery** [ˈhəʊziəri] a word used especially in shops for items such as tights or socks – 11 **sweatshop** small factory where people work hard for little money – 20 **to get to grips** to understand

With me though it was like open season. He'd hit me for asking him too many questions or for daring to say something back to him. One time, he'd clipped me round the head for having a go at Harry, and I had answered back calling him a 'bastard'. I got beaten that day with his old hockey stick that he kept under the stairs and I had to tell everyone at school that I had hurt myself playing football. He hit me all the time, sometimes I reckon just because I was in his range. It was either his fists or his feet or anything hard that came to hand. Not that I was that bothered by it. I mean, he'd been doing it since I was a kid and I just saw it as one of the daily hazards of growing up – trying to avoid getting hit. I did wonder though why he singled me out. Sometimes I thought it was because I was the youngest and other times I really thought that he hated me for some reason, only I was never told what it was. Maybe he could see that I was more influenced by the whole Western culture thing than my brothers had been. He definitely didn't like the fact that my best friend wasn't Asian. Either way, getting hit all the time made me feel an outsider and the feeling just got stronger as I grew older.

We lived on Evington Drive, in an area that was popular with Punjabi families. There were only three bedrooms which meant that I had to move out of my box room and in with Harry when Ranjit got married and his wife moved in with us. Ranjit and Jas got my old room, even though it only just had room for their bed, but that was their problem. They were the ones who had nicked my room from me.

Sharing a room with Harry was like my worst nightmare. He was fat and hairy, and had a horrible habit of leaving his dirty football kit, muddy boots included, all over the place. He only bathed every three days and in the summer the room stank of stale sweat when he'd been lifting weights. At night I used to pretend that he wasn't there by pulling the duvet over myself like a tent and reading by torchlight. Even then he'd throw things at me or call me a poof.

'What you wanna read for, man? Bloody Dickens – what are you, a *gorah* (white) or something? Read about bloody man's stuff, innit.'

I hated having no privacy, no time to myself that wasn't intruded on by a brother who still found fart jokes incredibly

---

8 **to be in sb's range** *(here)* to be close – 11 **hazard** danger – 27 to **nick** *(inf)* to steal – 33 **duvet** [ˈduːveɪ] a bedcover filled with feathers – 35 **poof** [pʊf] *(BE inf)* offensive word for a homosexual man – 38 **innit** *(BE spoken; from "isn't it")* used to emphasize what has just been said – 40 **fart joke** dirty joke

funny. He was so bloody thick, it was like talking to a gorilla sometimes. I hated him. And he'd turn up like a bad smell every time I wanted some peace, no matter where I was – the garden, the garage, wherever. Recently Ranjit and his wife had started doing the same, always around and giggling at each other like kids.

My mum was always in the kitchen, cooking, or watching the Asian channels on Sky in the living room. And Dad? Well, he was a law unto himself, walking round the house like a drunken zombie, belching all the time. To escape, I'd tried locking myself in the bathroom once but only succeeded in getting a smack in the mouth from him for my trouble. I couldn't even do my homework in peace because no-one in my family saw it as being important. They thought that school was a waste of time, like quite a lot of working-class Punjabi families. All they were interested in was trying to earn money and you couldn't do that at school or college. Ranjit and Harry had both got jobs in factories as soon as they left school. It was a wonder that I ever got the high grades that I did – not that anyone in my family cared.

I spent as much time as I could out with my friends. Adrian, my best mate who I'd met at junior school was, as he described himself, 'Black-Jamaican'. I spent most of my time outside the house, with him and some other lads. But mainly Ady. We played football together, for the school and on Sundays for a local youth club team. In school we were always together, meeting up during every break and having a laugh together. To my family Ady might as well have been the devil in disguise. They were always on at me about him, especially my brothers and my old man. I'd be at the front door, just about to escape and my old man would appear, pissed on Teacher's, at the living-room door.

'Come back, Manjit!' he shouted in Punjabi. I always knew what was coming so I'd make a face. 'Where you going?' Often he'd speak in this English–Punjabi hybrid that always made me smirk because it sounded so funny and then – CLIP! – my left ear would be stinging. 'Where are you...?'

'Out.' That's all I ever said to him.

'I'm not blind, Manjit, I can see that you are going out. Where to?'

---

1 **thick** *(here)* stupid – 10 **to belch** to let air from your stomach come out of your mouth noisily – 36 **to smirk** to grin

'Just up the road with Ady.'

'Ady? Bloody hell! Why are you always with that *kalah* (black)?'

And that would be it. I'd go mad because my old man was dissing my best mate. I'd call him a racist, get another clip across the head and then he'd pour out all of his prejudices about black people.

'You see if I'm not right. That *kalah* will lead you into drugs. I watch the news, boy, I know what these *kaleh* are bloody doing, taking bastard drugs. Bad society. You'll be stealing and smoking...'

I'd get another slap and then storm out of the house, with him swearing after me, shouting, telling me to be back for roti or else. As if he really cared. He would be drunk every night after work and all weekend, even though he pretended not to drink on Sundays. Most nights he would pass out by ten and forget that he wanted to beat me for coming in after I was allowed.

As for all that stuff about stealing and smoking, he knew *nothing*. In reality it had been me who had led Ady astray. I'd been the one who had started shoplifting at places like Boots and HMV, for deodorants and CDs and stuff. It was so easy that I'd got Ady to come along. We stole lipsticks, hair gel, all kinds of things – to order, selling them on at half-price to other kids at school. It wasn't even that serious. It was more a way of showing off, like smoking. We only did that to get in with the older lads or because we thought, stupidly, that it would impress the girls. I never even liked the taste. I suppose it was all part of growing up – being rebels.

Ady was well chilled out, like nothing ever bothered him or upset him, but in many ways he was also a lot like me. He lived with his mum and dad, who were educated and wanted him to do well at school. His brother was about five years older than us and he was a bit of a weed-dealer. Not much, just a few bits here and there. But Ady wanted to be like him and he had this thing about not doing what his parents wanted. Ady didn't even have a particular reason either; he just liked to play the bad boy which, at that age, was quite a funny thing.

I didn't care what anyone said about him anyway. He was my mate and we did everything together. My early adventures with

---

5 **to diss** *(inf)* to say unkind things about sb behind their back – 13 **roti** ['rəʊtiː] round flat Indian bread, also called *chapati* (*Fladenbrot*) – 16 **to pass out** to become unconscious – 19 **to lead sb astray** to encourage sb to do bad things – 20 **shoplifting** stealing from shops

Ady were a prelude to my future. Like a one-minute trailer to a film – a taste of what was to come.

Chapter Two
May

I was in Year 8 at school when the date for Harry's wedding was set. Within the year I was going to have to move into a new room that was being built as part of an extension to the house. My old man had planned it for years and had the money put by for it, having worked in the same plastics factory since he'd come over to England and saved every penny he could. In Punjabi society it is the custom for the bride to live with her in-laws as part of the extended family, but sometimes that meant having as many as three or even four generations of the same family living under one roof. Nightmare. That was the way I looked at it.

One of my cousins, Ekbal, who was the same age as me and went to a school only half a mile from mine used to talk to me about it – the extended family thing. He was my mum's nephew, her brother's youngest kid, only my dad didn't really talk to Ekbal's dad. Ekbal's old man was a doctor and he was the exact opposite of my old man, really forward-thinking and chilled out. Ekbal was allowed to do what he wanted within reason as long as he studied hard and made sure he went to university. His old man saw education as important and didn't mind what colour Eky's friends were. My old man called him 'Mr Professor', as though being successful was some kind of fault or handicap.

'Look at him,' he'd say after a couple of drinks. 'Who does he think he is, with his degree and his *gorah* language? Better than me? I am still a Jat Punjabi, not bloody English like him. When the *goreh* kick us out I will have land to go back to. What will he have? Never done a day's hard work with his computers and his desk. How will that help him in India?'

I always wondered why I'd ended up in such a traditional Punjabi family and not one of the more liberal ones. Eky was so lucky. My whole family life – it just seemed so claustrophobic, so unnatural. I couldn't imagine having to live like that. But then I didn't *have* to imagine, I would be going through it soon enough

---

25 **degree** *(here)* the title given by a university after a student has successfully completed a course of study – 32 **claustrophobic** [klɔːstrəˈfəʊbɪk] fearing small, enclosed spaces

and I was far from happy. As far as I could tell my new room was going to be the size of a broom cupboard, an afterthought, stuck next to the bathroom. I imagined myself stuck in there for years, locked away like a modern-day man in an iron mask (without the mask of course) as my family expanded mercilessly around me. They would remember me years later and discover me emaciated and unable to remember how to speak properly…

I got a bit like that sometimes, my mind raced off into the fantastical depths of my imagination, uncontrolled by reason or logic. Maybe I was just overreacting to it all. Maybe it wouldn't be that bad. But then I found out that Ranjit and Jas were expecting a little squealer and my whole world started to cave in.

I sat in my room one night, thankful that Harry was at football practice with the Bhangra and Bacardi posse, which was what I called his mates, writing out a plan of my life: a timescale that detailed the way I saw my life going over the next year. May right through to April – the month in which Harry was to get married and Ranjit's squealer would be gurgling through its fourth month on the planet.

MAY   HELL ON EVINGTON DRIVE
JULY SCHOOL HOLS BEGIN – POSSIBLE REDEMPTION?
SEPT YEAR 9 AT SCHOOL
      NEED MORE EXCUSES FOR SKIVING
DEC   THE SQUEALER ARRIVES
      HELL ALL OVER AGAIN
APRIL THE END IS NIGH
      HARRY GETS MARRIED
      BANISHED TO MY NEW CELL
      NO FUTURE

I sat on my bed and read it over. April next year. My life as I knew it would be over at the age of fourteen and a half – shut into my new room, a broom cupboard, as my family took over. Ranjit and Jas with their kid. Harry and his wife, who was going to need a highly underdeveloped sense of smell to be able to put up with his various odours. My mum, bragging to all my auntyjis about her grandson or granddaughter (a boy, of course, being the most preferable). And my old man, pissed and violent

---

5 **merciless** cruel – 7 **emaciated** looking very skinny after having starved severely – 12 **squealer** (here) [ˈskwiːlə] baby – 14 **posse** [ˈpɒsiː] group, gang – 22 **redemption** relief of a strong pain or rescue from a difficult situation *(Erlösung)* – 24 **to skive** *(BE, inf)* to avoid work or duty or, here school – 27 **nigh** [naɪ] near – 29 **to banish** to exile – 37 **to brag about** to show off *(angeben)*

as usual. Seven people in one house that had been specially revamped. Seven. Oh, and me too.

As I sat there and despaired for my privacy I heard Harry's heavy feet pounding the stairs. I shoved my timetable under the duvet just as the bedroom door flew open under my brother's shoulder charge. He seemed to be approaching seventeen as an overweight ape, complete with fur and fleas.

'What you doin'?' he smirked as he landed on his groaning bed with all the grace of a blue whale performing a belly-flop. I shrugged my shoulders at him.

'Nothing.' I looked at the duvet and then back at him.

'Nothing? You been up here for ages, Mummy-ji says, an' you're doing nothing?'

'Yeah,' I replied defensively. I didn't want him to find my timetable because he'd never stop having a go at me if he did. He looked at me and started to laugh to himself. Actually, it was more like a giggle.

'Bet I know what you been doing. Trying to tell me you been doing nothing, you little wanker.' He turned to the cassette player on our shared dresser, put in a bhangra cassette and pressed play.

'Frequent use of profanity is the sign of an inferior intellect,' I told him, repeating something Mr Cooke, my favourite teacher, had said to me after I had used the f-word once.

'Stop talking like you something special, you poofter. Speak normal. What you think you are, some kind of *gorah* or something? Anyone would think you was white, innit.'

I looked at him and screwed up my face. I hated the way my brothers spoke. Every sentence ended with 'innit' or 'wicked, guy'. They sounded like idiots. I was never going to end up like them, stupid and proud of it. No way. And whenever I showed the slightest inkling of brains, all they did was call me a coconut or some other such thing. 'Man, you're just a racist, Harry,' I replied, getting up to leave as the music began to irritate me.

'No, I ain't. I'm just proud to be Punjabi. At least I ain't ashamed, innit, of what I am and that. You always trying to be white, that's your problem.'

I glared at him, feeling this sudden urge to go and kick him in the head, the racist wanker. Instead I stormed out after calling

---

2 **to revamp** to overhaul – 8 **to groan** to make a long, deep sound *(stöhnen)* – 19 **wanker** [æ] (*BE taboo*) very bad word for a boy or a man who is thought to be stupid – 20 **bhangra** ['bæŋgrə] popular Punjabi form of music and dance – 22 **profanity** rude language – 25 **poofter** ['pʊftə] (*BE inf*) offensive word for a homosexual man – 29 **wicked** ['wɪkɪd] (*BE, inf, here*) excellent, cool – 32 **inkling** idea

him 'daddy's little robot'. I closed the door just as the trainer he'd picked up and thrown at my head hit it with a loud *thwack*!

One of the blessings of being part of such a big family, probably the only one at that, was that there were only so many seats in our car, a Vauxhall Cavalier complete with tinted windows and Sikh symbols in the rear window. Whenever one of my many cousins was getting married – and I'm talking a minimum of four every summer – my dad would pack the whole family into the Cavalier for the journey. When I was younger I'd have to sit on a knee or be squashed between my brothers and I would moan all the way about cramp and stuff. Now I was thirteen I was too big for that and ended up staying at home – not unsupervized of course. We had a nosy neighbour – another aunti-ji – who would keep an eye on me in between her shifts as the neighbourhood gossip. Most Punjabi weddings are three-day events and my parents usually went to the last two days, normally Saturday and Sunday which meant that I got one night to myself, every now and then, where I was left on my own to do the things that I wanted to do for a change – a really big thing for me.

Now you probably think that I used to go mad and invite all my friends round to the kind of party that you see the kids on *Neighbours* having. Well, sorry to disappoint, but I never did. My dad would have murdered me and that, *believe me*, is only a small exaggeration. No long lectures about trust. No getting grounded for two weeks. Just a straight beating, no questions asked. My reward was a simple one. I could watch *Match of the Day* without having to read the subtitles on teletext and without my stupid brothers farting and belching through it, drinking Carling Black Label like it was pop. And without having to watch my old man staggering around the room, ready to pass out, swearing in Punjabi at anything and everything.

If the football season was over I'd get out my *100 years of Liverpool FC* video and watch that, hoping that the following season we'd beat Man Utd for a change. After that I could turn off the lock on the Sky TV system and watch all the programmes that I wasn't supposed to watch – all the stuff that I wasn't even supposed to know about, like the porno on the Dutch and German channels and the horror films that always made me laugh more than they ever scared me. What I actually watched didn't matter. All that did matter was that I made the choices,

---

1 **trainer** (*BE*) sports shoe – 24 **to get grounded** to be kept indoors as a punishment – 30 **to stagger** to walk as if about to fall (especially when drunk) – 34 **Man Utd** Manchester United (a famous English football club)

just like the kids in *Lord of the Flies*, a book by William Golding that we'd read at school. I had the conch so I was in control.

Anyway, one Saturday in May, right at the start of my Schedule of Doom, my old man was getting everything together for yet another wedding trip, this time up to Glasgow. I was sitting in the lounge watching kids' TV and eating Frosties without milk, straight from the box. My dad walked in and belched twice. The sound echoed around the room like heavy thunder. I was so used to him doing it that all I did was pull a face and then carry on watching telly.

'Manjit,' he began, pointing to the cereal box. 'Getting bloody bowl for them.'

'Yes, Daddy-ji.' I always made sure that I was extra polite to him the morning after a real bender and using 'ji' after 'Dad' indicated respect for your elders and that was just what was required when he began one of his mega-hangovers. I went and got a bowl from the kitchen, but still didn't add any milk. On my return to the living room, my old man was sitting on the sofa, picking his ear with a forefinger.

'You don't want to come to your brother's wedding?' he asked, as I sat down and started watching TV again.

Through a mouthful of cereal I replied that he wasn't really my brother so it didn't really matter if I went or not. Bad move.

'You young people,' he said in Punjabi, 'what do you know? Brother, cousin, it's all the same to us. We are Punjabis, Manjit. Punjabis. Not bloody *goreh*...'

Here we go again, I thought to myself, as he began one of his tried and tested lectures about saving Punjabi culture from the grips of the white man and his filth, about being careful not to become too white for your own family.

'... put their own mothers in homes. At least we look after our families,' he continued. And then came the twist, stuck into the conversation like a knife, only casually. 'We are Punjabis and proud of it. Good Jat Sikhs from a good family. Look at your brothers. Ranjit is a man now, working and married to a lovely girl and Bilhar will be doing the same. Sikh girls, beautiful and pure. What is wrong with them? Tell me?'

I stared straight at the telly, trying to look right into the picture like there was something hidden behind it.

'And when you are Bilhar's age, you will do just the same.'

His age? But he was only just seventeen. SEVENTEEN! That gave me four years. Four! The thought hit me like a brick. I

---

2 **conch** a large spiral shell sometimes used as a horn – 10 **telly** (*BE inf*) television – 14 **bender** (*inf*) time when people drink a lot of alcohol

hadn't even had a girlfriend, never mind thinking about a wife. And I had all these things that I was going to do. I was going to be a top striker for Liverpool and score the winning goals in a league and cup double. I was going to be the first Asian pop star and write a bestseller, go out with supermodels and win an Oscar and stuff. Loads of stuff. *Loads*. None of which included getting married at seventeen to some girl who I didn't know. I mean, what if she had a moustache like my Aunt Sukhjit? No way! I tuned back into my old man's lecture.

'... my duty will be done and I can return home to India with my pride and my honour.'

I was really staring hard at the TV screen now, trying to pretend that I had imagined it all. That my old man was not actually in the room but still asleep. Or maybe I was still asleep and this was just a horrible dream that I was having. My old man rose up from his seat and broke my thoughts. He looked straight at me.

'Are you listening to me, Manjit?'

'Yes, Daddy-ji,' I replied, trying not to let him see my face. My mouth had started to get really dry and I could feel a cold sweat breaking on my forehead. I felt sick.

'Good. I have a friend whose daughter is only a few months older than you. She will be coming here on a visitor's visa and he needs to find her a husband so that she can stay in England. He is my good friend, Manjit, and I owe him a favour. But we will talk about this when the time is better. Not now.' With that he walked out of the room and left me sitting there in shock.

There had to be a way of escaping. There *had* to be. I even considered praying at one point, until I realized that I had never prayed in the past and that God was likely to know that I was trying to pull a fast one. No, there had to be a way out, a *cheat* like you get on all those computer games, a way up to the next level without losing too many lives. There had to be one, because in this game I couldn't just switch off the console and start again later. Man, this was deadly serious.

---

30 **to pull a fast one** *(BE, inf)* to trick or cheat

Chapter Three
July

The cheat kicked in some time in July and I started to go a bit wild. I can remember waking up one morning, I think that it was a Friday, and feeling as though I'd had enough. The shock of what my old man had said that day in May, about marriage at seventeen, kept on playing in my head like some silly Hollywood trailer. I needed distractions to stop myself thinking about being tied down at seventeen. I spent more and more time out of the house with Ady. We made our own distractions – and some just came along by themselves.

The sun was shining through the window of my shared bedroom and Harry had already woken and opened it, probably to let out the smell of his own feet. The sky was a really deep blue and cloudless and I looked down into the garden at all the flowers and shrubs that bordered my old man's lawn. I suppose that I should have been happy on a day like that but I had not been happy since my old man had outlined my future for me.

As I got up I stood on one of Harry's upturned football boots, right on the studs and stumbled backwards onto my bed. I sat there swearing to myself and rubbing my sore foot, looking around at the bombsite that was my bedroom. Harry's bed ran alongside mine, only a metre separating them. His bed was unmade as usual, the blue and yellow striped sheets badly needing a wash. It was covered in stained clothes and a few pairs of dirty off-white socks which stank. The metre-wide channel that ran between the two beds was a rubbish tip. Along with Harry's muddy, upturned boots were his shin pads; Manchester United shirt and socks; various cassettes and empty cassette cases, all featuring the latest bhangra artists; a plate with a half-eaten pakora sitting on it; a couple of glasses; cast-iron weights attached to a dumbbell; some of his magazines – all football, computer games and semi-nude women; a couple of empty CD cases and a CD that looked like it had been dipped in acid; the alarm clock that we had both got from yet another aunti-ji for Christmas two years earlier; *my* Liverpool shirt and, wrapped up inside it, an empty can of Carling Black Label.

---

14 **shrub** small bush, plant – 23 **stained** dirty – 26 **shin pads** hard covers you put around the lower part of your leg while playing soccer – 29 **pakora** [pəˈkɔːrə] *(Indian)* deep-fried piece of vegetable, chicken, etc served with a spicy sauce – 30 **dumbbell** two weights connected by a short bar, used for weight lifting – 35 **Carling Black Label** a popular brand of beer

I don't know whether it was the beer can that had stained my favourite football top, or just the general state of the rest of the room, but suddenly I started to get angry. I jumped off the end of my bed and opened my side of the cupboard which was built into the wall opposite the door. I pulled out a pair of black Levis and an Adidas top and put them on. Then I found Harry's favourite Man Utd shirt – an away strip from the previous season – and wrapped that around the beer can instead.

In my head John Motson screamed out, 'Owen gets his HAT-TRICK!' Scrunching the shirt up, I forced it under the bed with my good foot. 'And Owen gets ANOTHER ONE!!!' I put on a pair of black socks and my Nike Air Max before jumping onto Harry's bed, kicking his clothes and things all over the place. 'Surely he's not going to get another. HE IS!! FIVE GOALS FOR OWEN!!' Finally I got his half-eaten pakora, which was still covered in ketchup, and stuffed it into one of his empty cassette cases which I then put down on one of his pillows. On the cover some fat Punjabi bloke smiled out at me. Obviously enjoyed the snack, I thought to myself, as I jumped off Harry's bed and headed for the bathroom with John Motson going mad in my head. 'And Michael Owen has DESTROYED this Manchester United team...'

Throughout that summer break between Year 8 and Year 9 at school, I met up with Ady nearly every afternoon. I loved the fact that we always met down on Evington Road by St Philip's Church before heading off to wherever we were going. It was like a summer tradition with us and it got me away from my family.

One afternoon we were walking up Evington Road towards Victoria Park to meet up with some of the other lads in our school football team for a bit of a practice session. I didn't think that anyone was going to show up on that particular day because it was really hot but Ady told me that I was just being a pessimist.

I grinned at him. 'At least you're using that dictionary that your old man got you for Christmas.'

We walked up Evington Road past the Co-op and then stopped at an Asian-owned off-licence to buy a drink. The heat was mega but Ady still had a Chicago Bulls cap on his head, even though there was sweat trickling down the sides of his face.

9 **John Motson** English football commentator – 11 **Owen** (Michael Owen) famous English footballer – 39 **off-licence** shop where alcoholic drinks are sold (to be consumed somewhere else)

'Why don't you take that off?' I said, pointing at the cap.

'Nah, dready,' he replied, smiling. 'Not till I gets me a haircut, sah.'

'Yeah, but you're sweatin' all down your ugly face, man.'

'Oh, I loves the salty taste of me own sweat, my dear.'

I laughed at his change in accent from Jamaican to country bumpkin. He was funny like that; he could switch accents in an instant.

We walked on up the road as all around us the hustle and bustle of cars, buses, customers and shopowners continued. I was playing a game that I had invented called 'spot the white man'. The whole area was about ninety per cent Asian. All the shops were owned by Asians apart from a fish restaurant, a couple of hairdressers and a florist. Most of the people on the street were Asian too, or black. It was one of the things that I loved about Leicester. Some areas were nearly all white, some black and some Asian. And everyone kind of melted into the city centre so that it was all multicultural. I liked that – it was the way it should be – only it wasn't the way that my family saw it, or even Ady's when it came down to it. We used to say all the time, Ady and me, that it was down to us kids to sort things out. I mean, I was born in England. I liked being born in England. It was my home. If you stuck me on the streets of Delhi or Mumbai I wouldn't have a clue what to do or where to go. In England I knew how things worked. Man, England was my country and Ady's. Ours.

Ady broke my train of thought. 'Bwoi, it's getting to be like little Delhi round here, man.'

I just looked at him and grinned, suggesting that maybe the city council should change the name of the area as we passed by a pizza takeaway that included tandoori chicken, keema, and mutter paneer in its list of toppings – a clever thing to do in a mainly Asian neighbourhood, even though most of the shop's customers were white students.

As I crossed over Beckingham Road, halfway up Evington Road, I realized why I loved this part of Leicester so much. On the one side there was Highfields, an area that loads of people called the ghetto. I suppose a few parts of it were dangerous but mostly it got a bad rep because loads of black and Asian people lived there and all the racists couldn't handle that. There was this image of it as being full of drugs and prostitutes and gangs. Well, it had all of those things – but then so did lots of other areas

6 **country bumpkin** person from the country – 27 **bwoi** "boy" (in a pretend North American accent) – 39 **bad rep** bad reputation

of Leicester and if some of the people that slagged the place off ever actually bothered to go see for themselves, they would find big old houses, with huge cellars and attic rooms, named after Greek gods and stuff. I loved those old houses and the way the streets were so narrow, with the odd tree or shrub planted into the pavement. The streets were mostly quiet during the day too. Back when we were younger we played games like kerb-ball and knock-door-run around there.

On the other side of Evington Road the streets all ran up towards London Road, which led you into Clarendon Park and, further south, to Stoneygate, two of Leicester's posher areas. In fact, a lot of the houses in the posher areas, especially in Clarendon Park, were dead similar to the ones in Highfields, with the same narrow streets. The only difference was that Clarendon Park was much more middle class and had loads more white families living there which automatically gave it a better reputation in the eyes of some ignorant people.

That was what I loved about living where I did. Evington Road was like a fence that I could sit on. Each day I could make a choice about whether I wanted to jump over to the Highfields side or the London Road side. It was wicked because some days Ady and me would be messing about in the narrow back streets of the ghetto, and the next we'd meet Ben, Penny and Parmy up the London Road to play football or cricket on the hockey pitch they had up there, or cross into Clarendon Park so that we could go shoplifting at the Spar.

No-one turned up at the park, just like I'd said, so we decided to head into town. We'd given everyone about half an hour to turn up, standing in the gravel car park watching a gang of Asian youths sitting in their parents' BMWs and Golfs, the doors open and sound systems blasting out a mixture of ragga, hip hop, RnB and bhangra. Standing by a red Cavalier SRI was a local dealer, Bucks, doing good business in five- and ten-pound weed deals. Ady and me both knew him quite well because he sold stuff outside our school – not just weed, but computer games and mobile phones too. As we headed out of the car park I nodded at him and told him that Harry was still a fat bastard when he asked. Bucks had gone to school with my brother and I think they still went out drinking every now and then. I told him that I'd give his regards to my brother and then we headed down into the city centre, past all the offices and shops that line London Road.

1 **to slag sth/sb off** (*BE, inf*) to criticize sth/sb – 7 **kerb-ball** street game in which a ball is thrown against objects on the street and then caught – 11 **posh** elegant

We popped into a couple of record stores, not really staying for longer than a few minutes in each because we weren't looking to buy anything. All we were doing was loafing, just wandering about aimlessly, seeing if anything was happening, something which loads of kids in Leicester seem to have turned into an art form. There were kids on skateboards rolling by, young girls with toddlers, groups of youths in baggy, no-ass jeans and baseball caps, all eyeing each other. A typical school holiday thing. Man, half of them loafed about during term time too, in and out of the arcades and the shopping centre. As we walked Ady told me about a girl at school, Sarah, who wanted to go out with him. I didn't really know what to say about it, mainly because I didn't have a girlfriend – and I didn't really want one, either. I'd never even considered asking a girl out. In the end, just to shut him up, I told him that he should go out with her, which made him grin.

'You'll have to start calling me "the ladies' don" if I do,' he said, laughing at me.

'You ain't no don.'

'Number one in de area, boss.'

I laughed back and told him that his head was too big although, secretly, I was kinda jealous that some girl had shown an interest in him. I mean, that meant that I'd maybe have to get myself a girl too, just to even things up.

We were wandering up into Silver Street which led into a pedestrianized square when I saw Lisa for the first time. Ady pulled on my sleeve and pointed at two blonde girls who were walking towards us on the opposite pavement.

'That's her, man!' he said excitedly, pointing at the taller of the two. I was too busy looking at the other one. She was wicked. Long hair in ringlets, a deep tan and wearing three-quarter length black combats with a black vest top.

'That's Sarah.'

'Who?' I asked, not really paying attention to him.

'Sarah, man. The girl from school.'

'So who's the girl with her?' Man, I was in shock. I couldn't stop looking at her. And as they both passed by, they smiled. I mean, it was obvious that we were just gawping at them.

'Dunno, my yout', but you check that smile she gave me? Man, I'm in there.'

'They were smiling at me, bwoi. Not you.'

---

3 **to loaf** [ləʊf] to hang around – 7 **toddler** small child – 31 **ringlet** small curl (in hair) – 38 **to gawp** [gɔːp] to stare – 39 **yout'** youth, young man

'Yeah right,' Ady laughed. 'Because they really loved your Bollywood bad boy looks, innit?'

We didn't see them again that afternoon, but somehow I had gone from not being sure about wanting a girlfriend to wanting the girl with the ringlets in her hair in the space of about five minutes.

Chapter Four
August

I found myself thinking of the girl with the ringlets in her hair more and more, and I started to do stupid things – like shoplifting anything that I could lay my hands on. Both of those things were my way of putting the troubles at home to the back of my mind. I couldn't get Ringlets out of my mind and I just knew I had to see her again soon. In the end I almost engineered our next meeting.

I was with Ady and we'd been playing football on Victoria Park with some other lads from our school and my cousin Ekbal and his mates. When the game was over, I told Ady that we should go into town but he said he wanted to go home instead.

I really didn't want to go home. Not with the way things were with my family. After my revenge mission against Harry's CDs and stuff, he'd punched me and I'd threatened him with a knife. Just to scare him – I was never gonna use it – but Harry acted like the big kid he is and told the old man, who beat me up. I couldn't wait for the day that I would be old enough to leave home.

Ady finished his cigarette and flicked the butt high into the air. 'What we gonna do then?' he asked as I kicked at some gravel.

'Come on, Ady, let's go into town.'

'Man, we always go into town. Let's do something else.'

'Yeah, but we might bump into Sarah again. You'd be pissed off if I went into town on me own and saw her.'

'Who you trying to kid, rude bwoi? You only hopin' that she'll have that other girl with her. Ringlets.'

But I got my way. We walked into town along New Walk and on to King Street. I used to love some of the old buildings around there, the ones with their original shop fronts still intact. We stopped at a stationery shop and Ady got the look of a bad boy in his eye and decided he wanted to go in there. I walked across the road to look in the window of a small art gallery. There was a print in the window, a Matisse painting which I think is called 'Blue Nude'. I'd seen it in a book about famous artists that I'd borrowed from Evington library once. I remember thinking that this print would be the first thing I'd buy when I finally left home.

The door of the stationers' suddenly flew open and Ady ran out, clutching pens in one hand and holding onto his cap with the other. His bag was bobbing like crazy on his back as he ran. I watched as the old shop assistant hobbled out after him, shouting for him to stop. He was already halfway down the street by the time she got through the door. I shook my head as I set off after him.

'Was that worth the effort?' I asked him after we had bought a McDonald's and headed into town. We were only a minute's walk from the scene of the crime and Ady was proudly eyeing his goods. He just grinned and showed me the Parker fountain pen that took pride of place amongst his little haul. I had to admit it was a pretty cool pen, worth a bomb.

'I'm gonna sell it to Hital, man. He's always telling me to nick him one,' he said.

'How much?' I asked, realizing that if there was money involved, I might get a cut. We did that, Ady and me, shared the profits on most of the things we stole and sold at school. We had this deal about friendship first and everything else second. It seemed to work out pretty well too. Mostly.

'Let's see now. Twenty-two ninety-nine in the shop. Then there's all the hassle of nicking it in the first place, plus the spare cartridges that I got as well. I think fifteen 'pinds' for the lot should cover it.' Ady had put on a mock posh accent. 'What say you, Mr Merryweather?'

'Damn good business, what, Mr Farquar,' I replied, using the silly names we'd made up after watching the Harry Enfield Show.

Ady eyed the pen again before speaking again, now in his normal voice. 'Why Hital can't buy one is what I don't get. I mean the silly knob's loaded. His old man drives that Lexus and they got that big house in Oadby.'

'That,' I replied, 'is exactly why he's rich and we ain't. I mean, Hital's got more money than anyone else at school but he's tight with it. Has he ever let you have some of his drink? Crisps?'

'Now that you mention it, nah, he never has.'

33 **Harry Enfield Show** BBC comedy show – 41 **crisps** (*BE*) potato chips (*AE*)

'Exactly. Cause that's one of the ways that the rich stay rich,' I continued.

Ady gave me a mocking look. 'Oh yeah? Boy, ah sure'n hell as hope you ain't a goin' pinko on me now.' This time the accent was John Wayne.

'You know this street used to be called Cankwell and not Cank Street years ago?' I said, changing the subject. I'd read about it in some local history booklet at school. 'This bench we're sittin' on, it's right above where the well actually was.'

'I couldn't give a toss.' Ady threw his burger wrapping to the floor. 'Let's go check out the Shires.'

The Shires was the shopping centre in the middle of town. As with most afternoons there were gangs of young kids in there, wandering around taxing each other or bothering the security. I couldn't work out why Ady liked the place so much but he did. We always ended up in there.

'Man, we checkin' out de *honeyz*, innit?' Ady would say, putting on an accent that mimicked the way that lots of young Asian lads spoke in Leicester.

We were in there for about half an hour, wandering in and out of the shops not really looking at anything, before I spotted Sarah coming out of a clothes shop. I looked behind her to see if her friend was with her, the girl with the ringlets, and there she was, right on cue, carrying two bags with the shop's logo on them. I tapped Ady on the shoulder to get his attention. He was busy watching a couple of black girls walking in the opposite direction.

'What?'

'There they are.' I nodded towards Sarah, who saw us and smiled. She said something to her friend, who shrugged her shoulders and then they started to walk towards us. Ady saw them and started to straighten the cap he was wearing and then pulled up his jeans.

'Man, we is *in* here, bro',' he said in a stupid American accent. 'Yes siree.'

Sarah stopped in front of Ady and said 'hello', smiling at me when she'd finished. I must have gone a shade of red because Ady just started laughing and then Sarah joined in too. I looked at Sarah's friend who seemed to have gone as red as me.

'You're Ady, aren't you?' Sarah asked.

24 **on cue** promptly

'Yeah. But you know that already.' Ady was on the attack – the 'girls them Don' in action.

Sarah smiled at his reply and then turned to me. 'So who are you?'

I looked from her to Ady and then to Ringlets, who was even more gorgeous at close range. She had mad green eyes and her face was kind of catlike. This time she had on a pair of wicked Acupuncture trainers and grey combats, with a little white crop top, underneath which she obviously had nothing else on. Man, I thought I was gonna start stammering. 'Manny,' I managed to reply, but then my mouth just went numb and my brain died. I prayed that she wouldn't ask me anything else for a while. Even the palms of my hands had started to sweat a little.

'I think maybe we might buy you two young ladies a coffee or something,' began Ady, winking at me. 'After all, ain't like we're doing anything else this afternoon.'

'What, so we're like a stopgap?' asked Sarah, her face clouding over. I gave Ady a death glare. I mean what a stupid thing to say.

Ady picked up on it and started to backtrack. 'Nah, nah. That's not what I meant to say, man. What I meant to say was...'

Sarah looked at Ringlets and then straight at Ady. 'Gotcha. You're easy to wind up!'

Both of them started laughing as Ady realized they had just blown his 'Mr Cool' out of the water like a torpedoed submarine. I grinned too, which made Ady scowl.

'So where you taking us?' asked Ringlets, speaking for the first time. I looked at Ady and then back at the girls, rubbing my hands against the back of my jeans whilst my heart went haywire.

Chapter Five
October

By the time Year 9 began, Ady had started going out with Sarah and I had found out that 'Ringlets' was actually called Lisa, that she and Sarah were cousins and that she went to our school. I found it hard to believe that I had never noticed her before. Sarah had told Ady that she kept to herself for the first two years and that, although she didn't look it, she was actually a bit of a

---

17 **stopgap** substitute – 26 **to scowl** [skaʊl] to grimace, to pull a face – 29 **to go haywire** [ˈheɪwaɪə] (*inf*) to get out of control

swot. She had changed her hairstyle over the holidays and been to Turkey for a month which explained the suntan. Even so, I still couldn't believe that she had escaped my attention, even if she was part of the other half of our year and we never had lessons together.

I was really excited about starting Year 9, hoping that Ady could arrange for me to meet Lisa properly. Back in the summer when we had gone for coffee, we hadn't said much to each other, apart from little bits about what class we were in and stuff like that. I had the impression that she didn't like me but Ady told me that she was just like that. Kind of aloof. Every time I saw her in school I was tempted to go and say hello but she had ignored me so far and I was beginning to give up on ever being able to ask her out. Ady just laughed at me and kept on telling me to ask Lisa out. All you gotta do, he'd say, is just ask her out. That's all. Only I couldn't. On the one hand I was scared of making an idiot of myself by stuttering at the crucial moment. And then, what if she said no? I'd be well embarrassed.

On the other hand I really *couldn't* ask her out. I mean, what if she said *yes*. It meant getting involved in all the stuff that came with it, like phoning each other up every night. I couldn't risk one of my brothers or my father picking up the phone. They'd murder me. Imagine. A *girl*. *Calling* me. On *their* phone. It must sound stupid, but that was the way it was for me. You see in my parents' eyes it wasn't right, all this girlfriend/boyfriend stuff. They were *hyper*-traditional about it. The only relationship you could have involved marriage, otherwise it was a slight on your family's honour. You didn't go out with the kind of loose women that the Western world tempted you with. White girls. Black girls. And especially not Asian girls because that was even worse. Some families, like Eky's, had chilled out a bit over the whole issue, but not mine. In my house you had to just wait until *they* found someone for you to marry. After that you could do what you wanted. But not until then...

As for inviting her back to my house. No way! I'd probably just about get away with a girl phoning me. But only if it didn't happen more than once and even then only if I lied through my teeth about who she was and why she needed to talk to me about 'that science project' we were having to complete together. As part of a group, of course.

---

1 **swot** *(BE, inf)* someone who studies very hard and is not interested in other things apart from school – 11 **aloof** distant, unapproachable – 17 **crucial** [ˈkruːʃəl] extremely important

If I ever brought a girl home I'd be dead meat. My mum would probably start acting out some melodrama like the ones that she watches on Asian satellite channels. My dad would hit the roof, hit me, and then hit the bottle. And as for my brothers – well I just didn't want to think about it. They'd probably wolf-whistle and leer at her, make suggestive comments and ask me if I minded sharing. No joke. Once, when I was forced to go to the park with them, a group of young Asian college girls walked past us as we played with a football. Ranjit started whistling at them and Harry asked them all sorts of crude things in Punjabi before shouting '*Chok deh Phutteh!*' at them. It's the bhangra music equivalent to 'raise the roof' or 'take it to the bridge' or something. Only my brothers used it as a war-cry every time they saw their friends or when they wanted to harass some girls. That's what I mean when I say that I never want to end up like them.

Sometimes I used to dream that I was adopted. In the dream I would get home from school to find that my parents were waiting for me. My father would have a serious expression on his face, the one he wears when he thinks that he is being intellectual, like when he watches the news. My mum would be hiding her face from me, muffled sobs coming from her mouth. It was always the same. For some reason I'd be wearing Michael Owen's shirt, even though we aren't allowed to wear sports gear to school, and the telly would be on, showing some talk show on kids who divorce their parents. In his hands, my dad would be holding a piece of paper, my birth certificate. He'd look me in the eye and then shake his head. 'I do not know how to say this, Manjit,' he'd say. 'I am afraid that we are not your real parents.' I would look at him and then look at my supposed mum and I would laugh, not cry and call them liars and tell them that I hated them. No, I'd just laugh and tell them that I already knew. And then from behind me, the living-room door would open and in would step my real dad. Only in every dream he'd change. He might have dreadlocks and be a ragga superstar, or he'd be the owner of Liverpool Football Club; or some multimillionaire who had been on amazing adventures around the world. Whatever took my fancy. Anything but my actual father. And then the dream would end and I'd wake up to the smell of Harry's body odour, masked by cheap aftershave from Superdrug – *own label.*

---

6 **to leer** [lɪə] to grin, to sneer – 12 **to raise the roof** to make a very loud noise when singing and celebrating

All that was just a dream. In reality, I was just Manny – who couldn't ask a girl out, and whose best mate, Ady, did have a girlfriend.

One lunchtime Ady persuaded me to come out with him to see Sarah. I wasn't up for it, but Ady insisted and we set off on the bus. Sarah lived with her mum in a flat outside town. Her mum was at work so Maxine, Sarah's older sister, let us in. Maxine was Sarah's half-sister. Her father was black, whereas Sarah's was white. She had a kid brother, too, Mikey, who was half-Spanish. I suppose it was quite a mix, her family, but it didn't bother me. Our school was full of mixed-race kids and brothers and sisters who shared only a mum or dad in common. Or they were part of two families who had been thrown together. I thought it was brilliant, all that kind of stuff.

Ady and I went up to Sarah's bedroom, which was just about big enough for her bed and desk, never mind three people. We sat on the bed and she went to get us some Coke. Her room was covered in posters of boy bands and on her desk was a radio tuned to Radio One. I felt kind of stupid sitting there because she was Ady's girl and I was in the way. Ady didn't seem too bothered though. He was lying back, his head against the wall, covering Robbie Williams's face.

'You sure that you want me to be in here?' I asked him.

'Yeah. Why not, man? Ain't like me an' her's gonna get busy or anything. Not with her sister in the house anyway.'

That reassured me for a while, and when Sarah came back with the drinks we just sat and chatted. Me and Ady took turns to laugh at her tape collection. It was *bad*. No rap or ragga or anything. Just boy bands and other girlie stuff like *1200 Dance Anthems Part Six* or something. I didn't feel like a gooseberry because I was involved in the laughs. But then Maxine shouted up that she was going into town and I heard the door slam shut. Ady looked at me, as if to say go away, and I tried to think of a way to leave them alone. Three was now a crowd.

Then Sarah chirped up, 'Me mum's just had cable. We've got MTV and everything.'

'Can I go and watch it then, Sarah?' I asked.

'Yeah, if you want. It's already switched on. Just use the remote that's covered in plastic to flick channels.' I got up off the bed and left the room, feeling well embarrassed, and heard what they said about me as I went downstairs.

'You think he'll mind?' Sarah was asking Ady.

Ady laughed. 'Nah, 'course he won't.'

''Bout time he got a girlfriend, innit?'

'Yeah,' replied Ady, 'only I don't think he's got the nerve to ask *anyone* out – if you get me drift.'

'You on about Lisa again? I'll talk to her. She isn't seeing anyone either and I think they'd be good together. I'll have to put a word in.'

'So what did you and her get up to, then?' We were walking back towards my house. Ady wasn't saying anything. He just had this huge grin on his face. 'Go on Ady, man, tell me what happened.' I realized that I was begging for the information and felt stupid. 'Don't tell me then. Probably nothing anyway.'

'Nah, man!' My trick had worked quick time. Ady was on the defensive. 'We did nuff tings, man. Nuff!'

I just laughed at him as he tried to convince me that they had had sex.

'I'm tellin' you, Manny, it were wicked. We did it an' everything, man.'

'I don't believe you, Ady. You're just like a politician. Too lie.' I was speaking in my pretend black accent and I knew it was winding Ady right up.

'Nuh bother talk like fool, bwoi,' he replied, mimicking my mimic, 'me know seh yuh tink you is black.'

'Yeah, yeah, yeah. Like you really did it with her.'

'All right, all right, man. Me never really score the goal.'

'See? Yuh too lie, man.'

Ady grinned a wide grin at me. 'Me done hit the woodwork though!'

* * *

I got home well past six and my old man went crazy at me. 'We've been worried about you, out with that bloody *kalah* all the time. I have had to send your brother out to look for you.' That kind of thing.

Once my dad had finished ranting on I went up to my room to do some reading. Harry was out somewhere, so my evening was quite peaceful. I even got to play *my* music for a change, rather

---

5 **if you get me drift** (*BE inf*) if you get the meaning

than listen to all that bhangra and soul rubbish that Harry liked. It was almost heaven.

Unfortunately, Harry had to come back, putting an immediate stop to my peaceful night. He walked in, his heavy feet pounding the floorboards, and threw his jacket at my head. I said nothing as I threw it back at him. He grunted to himself and pulled my cassette out of the tape player.

'Watch what you do with that. It ain't mine,' I said.

'What is it – bloody black man's music?'

'You're an arsehole, man.' I couldn't understand how he could be such a racist. He'd probably never even made friends with anyone non-Asian in his whole life.

'Don't answer back, Manjit. I'm older than you, innit.'

'Not mentally.'

'Very funny. You think you're so cleverer than me, innit, like you're white or something?'

'At least I can speak English properly.' I was amazed at the way Harry spoke. It's not like we'd had a different education or anything. He was just too thick to learn anything.

'Go on speaking English, innit. See where it gets you. I ain't interested in *gorah* stuff.'

'Nah, 'course not. Wouldn't understand it even if you were.'

'Coconut, man. That's you, man. Coconut.' Harry looked at the tape in his hands. 'And this black rubbish...' He started pulling the tape ribbon out of the casing.

I jumped up to stop him, but he just held me off. I was well angry. The tape wasn't even mine. It was Ady's. 'Leave it alone!' I was jumping into him, trying to get to the tape.

He finished destroying it and then threw it on the floor. 'There, have it, you poofter.'

My brain went haywire. One second I was looking at the tape, lying on the flowery carpet, the next I was picking up the tape player and trying to smash it against Harry's head. I missed Harry and hit the wall with it. The casing on the back fell off and some of the buttons flew into the air. I didn't see the bedroom door open. I didn't see Ranjit come in either. I swore at Harry and then Ranjit dragged me out of the room.

'Easy, Manny. Easy. Calm down.'

'That fat...'

'Don't worry, I'll sort him out. But you still shouldn't try to hit him. We are brothers, us three. Punjabis, innit. We ain't supposed to fight each other.'

'If he's what being Punjabi is all about – man, I don't want it.'

'Don't be stupid, Manjit. How can you stop being what you are?'

'Yeah, yeah.' I pushed Ranjit's arms away and headed downstairs to make myself a sandwich.

Chapter Six
December

'I can't believe it took us so long to talk to each other properly.'

Lisa looked across the table at me. We were having a coffee in an Italian bar in town, on what must have been our tenth date. Ady and Sarah had been good to their word, introducing me to Lisa the week after I overheard them discussing my love life in Sarah's bedroom. We hit it off straight away when Sarah introduced us, because Lisa had been holding a copy of the same book that I was reading. Our first conversation was all about books that we'd both read and ones which we wanted to recommend to each other. I also found out that she was a mad keen Liverpool fan thanks to her mum who was from that city. Well, after that it was plain sailing.[17]

'I wouldn't have known what to say anyway,' I replied, tapping my cup. Lisa smiled and pushed my hand away from the cup.

'That's so annoying. What's the matter, do I make you nervous?'

'No,' I replied, really quickly before looking away.

'Is something wrong?' She looked concerned.

I started tapping my cup again and sighed. 'It's just this thing about not being able to have you over to my house because of my old man.'

'Manny, I told you the other day, it's not a problem. My parents would have no problem with you coming over to mine. Sarah and Ady practically live there.'

'What do they do – your mum and dad?'

'Mum's a teacher at a school out in Loughborough and Dad lectures at the university.'

'In what?'

'It's a mix of sociology and cultural studies – really interesting stuff.'

'I love all that kind of thing.'

---

17 **plain sailing** very easy

'Well you should meet my dad. He can talk for hours. I'm sure he'd love it if you were interested.'

'I'd like that.' I looked away again, hoping she wouldn't ask me about my parents but she had other ideas. I thought about what I wanted to say about my old man and my mum, not wanting to give too much away but something about Lisa made me tell her things that I'd never told anyone else apart from Ady, and sometimes not even him. In the end it all came out in a flood. I told her about my old man and his ideas about culture and tradition. About how racist he was and what he thought of my friendship with Ady. When I told her about his threat to arrange my wedding she took hold of my hand and held it until I'd finished talking.

I went on about my mum and the way in which she was this person that I didn't really know. She never asked me anything and never got involved, as if she had learnt early on not to question my father, being a good Punjabi wife and taking a back seat to her husband. I told her that I thought my mum's life was quite sad and that I spent hours sometimes dreaming that I wasn't really my parents' child. We talked all about my brothers, too, and then I told her in more detail about what my old man had said to me about getting married at seventeen. And all the way through, she held my hand and listened in a way that no-one had ever listened to me before.

We spoke for hours and I didn't get home until gone seven which upset my old man as usual. But I didn't really care by then. Being with Lisa made me feel like I was walking on a cloud and I found myself listening to sad love songs and imagining that the lyrics were written about us. Really sad shit. Every time anyone in my house shouted at me or had a go, I'd start daydreaming about her to shut them off, and for the first few months that we were seeing each other it was easy to do. I couldn't believe my luck. One minute I didn't have a girlfriend and the next I had Lisa, who couldn't have been more perfect if I had made her up. I told myself that it was the least I deserved, having her in my life, after all the crap I got from my dad. And she really began to make a difference which meant the whole world to me.

About two weeks after the date in the coffee shop my cousin Ekbal and his mum and dad came round to see us. I was up in my room when they arrived and Ekbal came straight up. I was sitting on my bed when he walked in and immediately I could tell he wanted to ask me something.

'Hey, Manny, is it true?'

'Is what true?' I said, looking up from my book.

'About you getting married?'

'You what?' I raised an eyebrow at him, wondering what he was on about.

'My dad was just on about it on the way over.'

'Eky, you ain't making sense, man. On about what?'

'He said that your dad has got some girl lined up for you, from India, and that he wants to get you sorted out as soon as you leave school.'

'He said something about it a while back but it wasn't anything serious. He just told me that was what he wanted me to do.'

'Man, I can't believe that. My old man would never think like that.'

'Well the old man can say what he likes. I ain't doing it anyway,' I said with false bravado.

'Yeah, like he's gonna let you. Come on Manny, even my old man is wary of him.'

'He's just traditional, that's all. When the time comes he'll just have to chill out. After all, it is three years away.'

'Man, you can't do it. You'll end up like your brothers.'

'No way, Eky.'

'Seriously though, you need to tell him straight. You know, about how you want to go to Uni and that, and be a writer.'

'He wouldn't listen, Eky. He'd just give me all that crap about being a good Punjabi.'

'My old man's Punjabi but he ain't nothing like yours.'

'Yeah I know. All those liberal parents out there and I get stuck with him.'

'Well if you ever wanna talk about it, give me a call, man. You gotta make sure you don't crack under the pressure.'

'I won't, Eky. Believe me.'

It was only after Ekbal and his parents left that I allowed myself to really react to what he had told me. If my old man and my mum were going round telling people what they had planned for me, then they were deadly serious about it. I mean, they weren't going to lose face over it, not their precious *izzat* (honour). And if they were deadly serious then I was in big

---

20 **wary** ['weəri] cautious, distrustful

trouble. Up until then I had let the whole arranged marriage thing bother me but in the back of my mind I had always believed that they weren't serious about me having to do it at seventeen. And it was still a long way in the future. What Eky had just told me made me see the light as far as my old man's intentions for me were concerned. I realized that I was going to have to go for it if I wanted all the things out of life that I'd always dreamed of. And there was Lisa to think of too. I wasn't about to let them mess up my relationship with her. No way.

There was only one thing for it. I'd have to make myself as unsuitable as possible. What father-in-law in his right mind would want a thief and a smoker for a son-in-law?

part two

a year later

Chapter Seven
December

The police kept me in an interview room as I waited for Ranjit to come and pick me up. A policewoman had told me that I was being let off with a warning because I had never been in trouble before. I think the store manager had wanted to press charges but the police had told him it wasn't worth the bother. All I'd stolen was an empty CD case and he had got that back.

I had been with Ady in the HMV on the High Street. We'd been skiving the afternoon lessons at school and I had seen a CD that I wanted. I'd thought that I'd been really careful, making sure that I wasn't being watched. I hadn't really noticed the nerdy-looking bloke in the next row of racks, the one that had turned out to be a store detective. He just hadn't looked the type. He'd been like some complete geek. Anyway, he'd followed me out and nabbed me as I'd waited for Ady. And the worst thing was that the case had been empty. I'd felt so stupid. When the store manager called the police I'd just bricked it. I was going to get *killed* by my brothers.

The drive home was silent. Ranjit talked to the policewoman for a while and then signed some papers. As we were walking out, he just shook his head. I was relieved that he hadn't gone mad right there, in the station, but I knew that he was upset with me. He looked almost disappointed, like I had let him down. Harry would be a whole lot different. I knew that he would be going on about how I had shown up the family and all that stuff. It just wasn't the right impression to make, not when his wife was so new to our family. *His* wedding had been a total nightmare – a horrible kind of dress-rehearsal for what my old man had planned for me that I could only endure by kidding myself it would never happen. But now I wasn't kidding myself. I knew that I was in big trouble, and my stomach was turning over all the way home until I actually felt like being sick.

'Why you always trying to mess up the family's name?' The first person to explode, as soon as I got in, was Harry. I got two slaps across the face and then the shouting began. He was swearing at me in Punjabi, calling me all sorts of things and using words that he'd never dare to say in front of the old man.

---

4 **to press charges** to tell the police that you want a person to be taken to court (*Anzeige erstatten*) – 14 **to nab** *(here)* to catch someone doing sth illegal – 16 **to brick it** *(BE. inf)* to get extremely nervous – 27 **dress-rehearsal** last practice before show – 28 **to endure** to bear

'Daddy-ji goes to India because our aunty is dead and you think it's OK to go stealing with that black bastard!'

I wasn't going to back down. Not to Harry. I swore at him, told him to eff-off. I was fuming, tears flowing down my face. 'Get lost! I don't have to take anything from you, you fat bastard!'

'You ain't going out any more, not with that bloody *kalah* or anyone.' Harry looked to Ranjit for support, then laid into me a couple more times. Not that it bothered me any more. I had been slapped and punched that many times that it no longer even hurt. The more that he hit me, the angrier it made me.

'Leave him now, Harry. He's had enough, innit.' Ranjit had decided to speak up. 'Let me deal with it. The responsibility's mines.'

I wanted to laugh at the way he had said 'mines' instead of 'mine', but I didn't. I watched Harry sit down and measured up a kick at his head. Before I had the chance to go through with it though, Ranjit had grabbed both my arms, holding them in front of me.

'Get to your room, now!' His face was red and he spat the words at me.

'Get lost! You ain't my dad!' I tried to struggle free, but his grip was too strong.

'Get upstairs! Go!'

Jas and Baljit, Harry's wife, had been watching everything, wide-eyed, but had said nothing. Now Jas put her hand on Ranjit's arm, trying to calm him.

'*Chadd deh*. Let him go, Ranjit.'

'No, Jas. No way. He needs a lesson learning, innit.' Ranjit pulled me to the living-room door. 'Upstairs!'

I kicked at him and then ran upstairs, slamming my door shut behind me.

Ranjit came up to my room about an hour later and sat at the end of my bed whilst I pretended not to notice him. I didn't want to talk to anyone – at least to no-one in my family. I wanted to be with Ady, out on the streets, having fun and not thinking about crap all the time. But he wouldn't let up, asking me over and over about what was going on in my head. About what was wrong with me. I let him carry on until I started to cry and he came over and put his arm around me, which felt really strange because it was the kind of affection my parents hadn't shown me since I was a small child.

I let him hold me for about a minute before I started to feel embarrassed about crying in front of him. I pushed his arms away and shouted, 'I'M ONLY FIFTEEN AND I'M NOT GETTING MARRIED AT SEVENTEEN! I'M NOT! IT'S TOO YOUNG AND I WON'T DO IT. THE OLD MAN CAN KILL ME IF HE WANTS – I WON'T DO IT!'

Chapter Eight
May

'It is about time you started thinking about your future, Manjit.'

My dad was sober because it was Sunday afternoon and he had been to the gurudwara. Like a lot of other Punjabi men, he didn't drink or eat meat on Sundays. It was like some kind of religious fashion statement that he was making, only he generally tended to get even more plastered on Saturday nights to make up for it. I just thought that it was so stupid not to eat meat or drink booze on only one day in a week. What was the point? The way I saw it, you either were religious or not. I was sure it wasn't supposed to be something you made up for yourself. That was why I always tried to get out of going. Eventually my old man let me stay at home – not that he was even a Sikh. He was a Punjabi first; the religion came second. One was the way he actually lived his life, and the other was the religion he pretended to practice on Sundays. Not that I said any of this to my old man. I had gone through enough grief over the shoplifting thing; Harry had told him about it almost as soon as he had come in through the door back in January.

The old man's reaction had been like a bomb going off. No-one had escaped the fallout. Even my mum had got shouted at for not bringing me up in the right way and being too soft on me. My old man had had a really strict upbringing. My grandfather was in the Indian army and he had made my dad and his five brothers run five miles each morning before they went into the fields to turn the soil using ploughs that were harnessed to water buffalo. We had a lot of land and half was kept for growing corn whilst the other half was paddy fields of water and rice plants. That whole way of life shaped the way that my old man thought about everything. The way that he saw it, he had been

---

14 **booze** [buːz] *(inf)* alcohol – 18 **eventually** [ɪ'ventʃəlɪ] in the end *(schließlich)* – 32 **plough** [plaʊ] equipment used in farming to turn the soil *(Pflug)* – 32 **harnessed** ['hɑːnɪst] tied – 34 **paddy field** field in which rice is grown in water

made to work hard from an early age, and that was the best way to bring up a kid. Hard work and strict discipline. It was one of the reasons he disliked Ekbal's old man so much – because he saw him as soft.

When Harry told him about me and the shoplifting, it was like I had challenged his whole way of life – all his beliefs about what was right and wrong. And he had taken it out on everyone in the house. By the time he had finished he had made me feel like a leper. No-one in the house would talk to me or come near me. I began to realize what it must feel like for all those homeless people that we saw in town on Saturdays.

Now, this Sunday, the old man button-holed me as I sat on the sofa, my eyes glued to the live football game on the TV. Liverpool were at home to Spurs and Robbie Fowler had just missed a sitter. The game was really open, end-to-end stuff, but I could feel my dad and his bloodshot eyes glaring as I tried to keep my mind on the game.

'Manjit, I am talking to you.' His voice was super-calm, which was a pleasant surprise.

'Yes, Daddy-ji,' I replied, as Michael Owen went on one of his runs, dribbling past the Spurs midfield with ease. We were going to murder them. No problem.

'I have spoken to a friend of mine in India, about his daughter.' He paused for a moment. I think maybe he was waiting for me to say something. To react. But I just kept my eyes on the game and wondered what he was going to say next, about what he had agreed with his friend in India. I knew that it had to be about marriage because it had been exactly the same when he had told Harry.

We had been in the back garden playing Badminton with this cheap £9.99 set from Argos; it had a net that you tied to sticks. Harry had been getting all upset because I'd been making him look like the big whale that he was. He'd been all sweaty and out of breath when my dad walked up and told Harry that he was going to get married to the girl whose photo he had seen the week before. Just like that. My dad had already sorted everything out. They'd shown Harry a photo of the girl, dressed up in traditional gear and wearing too much make-up, then told him that it was *his* choice. They wanted *him* to make a decision – yes or no. It was all a con really. Harry didn't really have a choice,

7 **to take sth out on sb** to treat people badly although it is not their fault – 9 **leper** ['lepə] *(here)* a person who is avoided by others because he/she has done something shocking or bad – 13 **glued** [gluːd] fixed – 15 **to miss a sitter** (football) to miss an easy goal – 40 **con** swindle

or the opportunity to say no. All the decisions were made for him by my dad and the girl's father. Harry had known what his answer *had* to be. And, for Harry, it was probably the only way he'd ever *get* a girl, anyway.

Thing is, I was totally different to Harry. Totally. And there was no way that I was going to say 'yes' to marrying some girl from India just by looking at a photo of her. No way. So I began to concentrate really hard on the football, even though my mind was all over the place, and much of what my old man said at first went in one ear, and straight out the other. I was hearing but not listening.

I managed about five minutes before the old man's words started to cause my stomach to turn over. He was talking about *me*. And some *girl*. *From India.* He already had it all sorted out just like it had been with Harry. All that remained was the wedding itself. She was six months older than me and coming over to England on a visitor's visa in July. Two months away!

'I have told her father that you will marry her after next summer, when you are both seventeen. If we leave it any longer there will be too many questions from the immigration people. Once you are married she will have the right to stay in this country and I will have my final daughter-in-law.'

The look on my face must have said everything that I was thinking. My palms were getting all sweaty and I wanted to get out of the house. Just run. Be anywhere but where I was at that moment. I wanted to scream at him and shout and swear. Hit him. But I couldn't do anything. My legs felt like they were frozen, like two sausages waiting to be defrosted. My mind was all jumbled up and I kept on hearing this ragga tune that Ady had about being locked up in prison for a crime that I didn't commit. If I hadn't caught myself, I think that I would have ended up humming the melody out loud. And then, to top it all, Spurs scored to make it one–nil. It was like a sign. I was in trouble.

My dad obviously saw my reaction because he changed his lecture to one about how it was my duty to uphold his honour, his *izzat*. To protect the family name and all that.

'I do not want to be like the other men that they laugh at in the gurudwara: the ones whose sons and daughters have run away and become druggies and prostitutes, or married unsuitable people – Muslims and Hindus and *goreh* or, God forbid, *kaleh*. That is not why your mother and me brought you on to this earth. To ruin our name and rubbish our *izzat*. We brought you up to be a good Punjabi. And I won't let you ruin it all because you think that you are something different from us. Something special. Blood will always be blood, Manjit. And your colour will always be your colour. Look in the mirror. You are a Punjabi, not a *gorah*. You are not from this country, even if you were born here. These people are not the same as us. They are not the same. We have to protect our culture, Manjit. Our way of life.

'And do not think that I am stupid, Manjit. I have seen the way that you have been headed recently. Stealing and messing about at school. I found a cigarette in your room last week, too. You think that I will let you carry on this way? Ruining my name. No!'

I could see the anger beginning to rise up in him, like he was about to explode. His face was going red all over and the little blood vessels that he had on his cheeks and over his nose, from being an alcoholic, were showing more clearly than normal. My mum had come into the room and she sat down opposite me. I could tell from her face that she was about to launch into the kind of hysterics that she had gone into with Harry, emotional blackmail before he said 'yes'. And he had *wanted* to have an arranged marriage. Just to get a girl.

'Your poor mother has cooked and cleaned for you all these years. Wiped your backside and fed you. Think of her when you are out with that *kalah* of yours, smoking and chasing dirty white girls. Think of her and what the neighbours say to her when they see you walking around on Evington Road like a tramp. A criminal. Smoking your cigarettes in front of our relatives and friends, with no shame. What do you think you are, Manjit? Why do you think that I will let you be the one to ruin our name, when all of your brothers and sisters have not? *Das mehnu* (tell me)? Why? Do you want to kill me? Is that it? Do you want to kill your mother?'

Almost right on cue, my mum started crying and calling out to God. It was all 'Hai Rabbah' (Oh God) and slapping her thighs the way that Punjabi women do at funerals. I already knew that she was gonna do it – knew that she was just putting on an act to scare me into accepting their way of doing things. But even knowing this, seeing my mum crying and wailing made me feel guilty and upset, just like I was supposed to. My dad just carried on having a go at me, telling me that he was going to pull me out of school and send me to India until I agreed to do as they

20 **emotional blackmail** making another person do what you want them to do by making them feel guilty

said. And my mum just cried. In the end I ended up crying too because I didn't know what I was going to do. I felt like I was stuck. Like I had no choice. I mean, how could I become the cause of so much grief and sadness for my parents?

How could I?

Chapter Nine
June

Two weeks after that afternoon I found myself sitting in the classroom of the head of Year 10, Mr Sandhu. It was lunchtime and outside the sun was shining. It was hot for early June and we were about a week and a half from the summer holidays. I could hear all the other kids outside, messing about and having fun. And I was stuck in a stuffy classroom, waiting for Sandhu.

He had sent a Year 8 kid into my English lesson to tell me that I had to see him during the lunch break. It was a welcome distraction because we'd been studying World War One poetry. Some bloke called Wilfred Owen. Talk about boring.

Mr Sandhu was a proper tyrant. A teacher who ruled the classroom with fear. He was one of the deputy heads, so he was always banging on about standards and uniform and stuff. And he lost his temper really quickly, over the smallest things. He was also the school trouble-shooter. The one who told kids that they were being suspended or expelled. We were supposed to be like some football team, us kids, all pulling in the same direction. Sandhu, he was like the headmaster's sweeper – the one who cleared up all the loose balls that slipped through the net.

At first I thought I was going to get suspended but I hadn't been in trouble for at least a couple of months and, even then, it had been nothing major. Just a scrap with a Year 11 who had been bullying me and my friends. No, it was obviously about something else. Maybe something had happened to my family or one of my friends? What if he was to tell me that my entire family had died in a car crash? Sitting there, listening to the noise from the playground, my imagination created little images: me at my entire family's funeral, crying; then me, back at home, having the run of the place, with no-one to watch over me or tell me what to do; me doing an interview with the *Leicester Mercury* about the terrible tragedy. After a while I began to feel

---

15 **Wilfred Owen** British poet (1893-1918) – 17 **deputy head** vice headmaster, assistant principal – 21 **to suspend** to make sb leave school for a short time as a punishment – 30 **entire** [ɪnˈtaɪə] whole

ashamed of myself. My family had all been killed and I was daydreaming about how that would lead to the freedom that I always wanted.

It was while I was feeling guilty and asking myself if serial killers began their lives daydreaming about the death of their families that Sandhu walked into the room with a cup of strong-smelling coffee in a Leicester Tigers mug. He put the mug down on his desk, walked up to the table that I was sitting at and pulled up a chair. He was so close that I could smell the coffee on his breath. He looked out of the window and ran his fingers through his grey hair.

'Well, Manjit,' he began. 'I suppose you are wondering what I wanted to see you about?'

I shrugged my shoulders. I was looking at him and then looking at the clock above the classroom door, hoping that he would get on with it. I wanted to go outside and chill with Lisa. Our time together in school was precious to me because I was going to have to do some real serious storytelling to my old man to see her over the summer. Over a year together and still I had to lie about her all the time.

'I have had it brought to my attention,' Sandhu continued, 'that your performance in school is dropping. Your form tutor has picked this up from one or two of the other teachers. Are they right, hmm?'

'Dunno, sir.' I shrugged my shoulders again.

'Oh come along, Manjit, you do not need to play ignorant with me. We both know that you are an intelligent young man. Surely you can stretch your vocabulary to more than "dunno". Hmm?'

It was hard to work out what was more irritating about Sandhu. The typically Indian way that he pronounced my name, so that the 'jit' sounded like 'jeet', or the way that he finished every sentence with 'hmm'. I was really tempted to tell him to stick his vocabulary but my head told me to play along. My cheat didn't go as far as getting myself thrown out. Sandhu got up and fetched the mug from his desk. As he sat down again, the smell of the coffee made my stomach turn.

'Sorry, sir.'

'That's better, hmm? Well, what do you think, Manjit. Has your performance dropped?'

'How do you mean ... sir?'

'Well, up until last year you were one of the top students in your year group. We had you in all the top stream classes, did we not, apart from possibly Maths, hmm?'

'Yeah...? I mean ... Yes!' I corrected myself real quick.

'What we would call a promising student. On course for As and Bs across the board possibly. I know that you have a particular dislike for Maths, Manjit, but certainly you are good enough in all the other areas. Or rather you were, hmm?'

'Suppose so, sir.'

'You see, after your tutor – Miss Jones – expressed her concern to me, I had a word with all of your teachers. What they told me, Manjit, was not very good.' He was looking straight at me now, his eyes fixed on mine. But he wasn't getting angry at all. If anything he looked kind of concerned. Sandhu! Concerned. I had to be tripping.

'How do you mean, sir?'

'Well, let's put it this way. You are half way through your GCSEs, Manjit, and your predicted grades, if we did them today, would be as follows: English, Lit and Language, D stroke E, and that is probably your strongest subject. Sociology, D. Sciences, E. History, D. And so on. Somewhere between leaving this school at the end of Year 9 and going through Year 10, you have managed to slide from the very promising into the below average. And so I have had to ask myself why? It certainly isn't because the work is any harder. And you cannot suddenly have become far less intelligent than you were nine or ten months ago, hmm?'

I looked at him straight in the eye for as long as I could manage before I had to look away. What was I supposed to tell him. The work wasn't any harder. It was almost too easy for me. It was just that I couldn't be bothered with it. All I thought about was that dreaded arranged marriage and how I could escape it and live happily ever after. How could I tell him that? He was Asian himself and probably the same kind of age as my dad. He probably had the same views and everything.

'Is there a problem with the work, Manjit? Or something else in school that you aren't telling me about?'

'No, sir, not at all.'

'Are you being bullied, Manjit? By one of the older pupils?'

'No way, I ain't scared of any of Year 11.'

'But you had that trouble recently, hmm, with Manish Kotecha in 11CM. Is that all finished with?'

15 **to trip** to be on drugs – 18 **GCSE** General Certificate of Secondary Education, exam taken by English and Welsh children at the age of 15 – 19 **Lit** short for literature

I wanted to laugh when he said that, but I held back. Manish was the Year 11 who had bullied me and Ady since we had first come to the school. When we'd been younger we'd hide from him and stuff. But I was the same height as him now and he'd stopped looking so scary. If anything me and Ady were now bullying *him*.

'That's all over, sir. Manish doesn't bully me any more.'

Sandhu looked thoughtful, like he was trying really hard to work out what the problem might be. He had his chin in one hand, and was flicking the nails of his other hand against the coffee mug. I watched him do this and wondered whether he already knew that it was something else, my problem. Maybe he had guessed?

'So you are not the subject of bullying. The work is not too difficult for you. Yet your standard of achievement when you are in school is well below that which you are capable of. And your record of unexplained absences continues to grow.'

'Yes, sir.'

'Tell me, Manjit. What do your parents think of your relationship with Lisa Jenkins...?'

Chapter Ten
June

'He asked you what?' Lisa looked really shocked when I told her. 'How did he know about us?'

'I don't know. He's probably seen us together around school. It's not like we hide our relationship. He wasn't having a go at me or anything. He was concerned.'

It sounded amazing but it was true. Sandhu knew that I was having problems at home. He'd asked me about Lisa and how my parents were about it. When I told him that they didn't know about her, he just laughed and started banging on about the generation gap and the pressures of being young and Asian in Britain.

'He was talking about the difference in culture and things like that. He said he understood all about it.'

'So did you tell him about the way your parents are forcing you to have an arranged marriage?'

'A little bit. I just told him that my parents expected me to be something I'm not and about how they think school is a waste

---

30 **generation gap** a term that describes the difficulties and lack of understanding between the generations *(Generationskonflikt)*

of time. And the craziest thing is that he's married to a white woman.'

'Who? Mr Sandhu?' Lisa looked amazed.

'Yeah, told me himself. Says that if I think it's hard now, imagine what it was like for him in the 1960s.'

'I don't think I want to. Some of the looks I get when we go into town are enough. Aren't people really strange?'

'No, some of them are just stupid and can't see past what colour a certain person is.'

'I'm glad my parents aren't like that.' She looked at me with her bright green eyes and then looked away in embarrassment. 'I don't mean that I'm glad that your parents are like that. It's just that...'

'Hey, chill out. I know what you mean.'

We were sitting on some steps that led up to the tennis courts during the afternoon break. Ady wasn't in school, or at least no-one had seen him. He had been hanging around with his brother quite a lot recently, and I hadn't really heard from him. Knowing him, he was probably with Sarah somewhere, listening to underground garage music and talking rubbish with his cap on back to front. I realized suddenly how much I missed him and decided to try and call him. As I thought about him Lisa gave me a peck on the cheek and the teachers came out to round up everyone for the last lessons of the day.

'My mum's picking me up after school. Are you going to wait for me and get a lift home?'

'Will that be all right with her? I don't want to be a bother to her.' Lisa knew I wasn't telling the whole truth – she knew I couldn't have my old man see me pull up in a car with two white women. He just wouldn't understand.

'Of course it's all right. Meet you outside at four.'

* * *

While we waited for Lisa's mum after school, I talked a little more to Lisa about the whole deal to do with arranged marriages the way my parents saw it. Lisa told me again to say 'no' and to keep on saying it until my parents gave up.

23 **peck** small, harmless kiss

'They can't make you do something you don't want to do.'
'I know that. It's just that I can't say no. I've tried.'
'So just keep on trying until you get through to them. Talk to them.'
'You don't understand, Lisa. It isn't that simple. The girl I'm supposed to marry is going to *be* here, and my old man is threatening to take me to India if I don't agree. My mum just cries every time we talk about it.'
'So what are you gong to do? Say yes to keep them happy? What about what *you* want?'

That was the problem. I knew that I didn't want to get married young to some girl who I didn't even know. I didn't want to end up like Ranjit and Harry, doing that whole wife and kids thing. I didn't want to spend my life looking after my parents in their old age and having to go to the weddings of distant cousins because it was the right thing to do. I knew what I *didn't* want to do. It was just that I didn't know what I actually wanted *to* do. And deep down inside I was scared that if I did say no, my dad would kill me and my mum would kill herself as she kept on threatening to do, because of the shame. How could I do that to them? How? And how was I supposed to explain that to Lisa who was never going to have to choose between what she wanted out of life and her family? She didn't have to fight to be seen as an individual.

'I told you what they've been like. All my mum does is cry, starts slapping her thighs and threatens to *kill* herself.'
'But she did that with your brothers too. And you know that she doesn't mean it, don't you?'
'Yeah, but what if she does?'
'She won't, Manny, I promise.' She held my hand and squeezed it real hard, trying to reassure me. 'It'll be fine after a while. When they've accepted you for you.'
'I really don't think that will ever happen, Lisa. They're just too set in their old ways to accept what I want to do with my life. They'll just see it as a slap in the face.'

Lisa kissed me on the cheek and squeezed my hand again. I looked at her and tried to smile. She managed a smile for both of us.
'On a more selfish level, what about me?'
'You know how I feel about you, Lisa.'

---

31 **to reassure** to make sb less frightened

'And you know that I love you too. But if you end up having an arranged marriage, provided we're still together at that point, are you going to just cast me aside?'

This time I kissed her, on the lips and gave her a big hug. 'Never. And we will still be together – I know we will.'

'Oh Manny, what are we going to do?'

'We'll just *un*arrange the marriage.'

Lisa's mum pulled up as we were kissing. I pulled away in embarrassment but Lisa took hold of my hand again and led me to the car, a metallic blue Vectra with a diesel engine. Lisa's mum brought down the driver's side window and smiled out at me.

'Hi, Manny. Jump in!'

I'd met Lisa's mum – Amanda, as she liked me to call her – several times before and this certainly wasn't the first time she'd given me a lift. Sadly, she too knew the way my old man was about my going out with Lisa. She wasn't happy about the situation, but she had said it was something for Lisa and me to sort out – not her business.

Lisa turned to me. 'Can you come for dinner?'

'Nah, I'd better get home. I've got loads of homework to do and then there's what my old...' I started to say it but I always felt embarrassed about it in front of Lisa's mum. Lisa saved me again. She squeezed my hand and opened the rear door of the car.

'Come on, get in and we'll drop you off at the bottom of your road.'

I just looked at her and nodded and suddenly hated the way I had to sneak around in order to be with the girl that I loved...

I didn't speak again for the rest of the way home.

Chapter Eleven
November

I started Year 11 badly, not paying attention to the work or to the teachers; or to the two sessions that I had with Mr Sandhu in which he tried to get me to confront my problems. I couldn't take all that stuff seriously. I felt like one of those stupid American

---

3 **to cast sth/sb aside** to get rid of sth/sb because you do not need it/them any longer – 29 **to sneak around** to go somewhere or do something quietly and secretly

kids on the *Ricky Lake Show* – you know, the ones that want to divorce their parents. Sandhu was like, let it all hang out, let your feelings out – like some old hippie. Not me. Not with him. And most definitely not in school. No way. I didn't need therapy, I just needed out of my whole family.

I had seen as much as I could of Lisa over the summer, spending time with her family instead of mine. And increasingly I spent lots of time after school, once term had started, sitting with Lisa and her dad's old vinyl jazz collection, getting into Miles Davis and Wayne Shorter. I also started to skip lessons to see Ady and go into town, stealing money from home so that I could afford it.

And then I got put on an attendance report – about a month before my sixteenth birthday. It began with my skiving a PE lesson so that Ady and me could go into town for a coffee. After that I began to skip afternoons on a regular basis, taking money out of Ranjit's wallet so that Ady and I could have lunch or buy CDs and stuff. It took the teachers about five whole weeks to work out that I wasn't suffering from a chest infection or vomiting up a bad sandwich every other afternoon. The thing is, by that time they had already caught and expelled about eight other kids for skiving.

Ady had been the first one out, which was quite funny, because he wasn't actually in school when they expelled him. It was done in something called 'absentia' which Mr Cooke explained. He was all right, Cooke – the only teacher who I really liked or respected. Ady's leaving wasn't a shock. After all, he was never in school. In fact, I saw more of him outside of school than in it. The football team went right down the drain though – it just wasn't the same without our little partnership.

Eventually I got called into the principal's office and put on the attendance register. Nightmare! I had to sign in with one of the senior teachers in the morning, at lunch-time and at home-time. I was given three chances. If I missed three signings, that was it. Out the door. And to top it all I was kicked out of the footie team too! I began to miss the freedom that skiving gives you, even though it meant that I saw more of Lisa. Lisa wasn't happy about skiving; she thought I was attacking the wrong target, even after I explained my whole 'cheat' thing to her. In

---

10 **Miles Davis** (1926-1991) American jazz musician – 10 **Wayne Shorter** (born 1933) American saxophone player – 10 **to skip lessons** to play truant *(schwänzen)* – 13 **attendance report** record of how many times a pupil has been absent from school – 20 **to vomit** ['vɒmɪt] to expel contents of stomach through the mouth *(sich übergeben)* – 29 **to go down the drain** *here* to lose – 36 **footie** *(BE inf)* ['fʊti] football

fact, at one point it nearly split us up because she wanted me to do well at school and I just couldn't be bothered. Scared that she would dump me, I began turning up every day and, for a month, I didn't miss a single signing-in time.

My attempt at being a model pupil had to end, though. One night, just before my birthday, I was sitting in my bedroom at home playing one of those stupid computer games where you collect coins and sweets and stuff on different levels, getting really worked up because I couldn't get to the next level, when Ady rang up.

Ady told me about some night at a bar in town, and did I want to go? It was on all night and his brother was working on the door, so we could get in for free. Could I go? The grief that I'd surely get would be unimaginable. But, having said that, I found out that only Jas and Baljit, Harry's wife, were at home. I could probably get out and they'd get the blame if I was found out. And if I left my bedroom window open I'd be able to climb on to the low roof of the kitchen extension and sneak back in...

'What about the cheat, man?'

'What?' Ady had interrupted my thoughts. What cheat?

'Your cheat, my dan. Y'know, about being a bad bwoi to avoid the dreaded arranged marriage.'

'What about it?' I questioned him, but my brain had actually clicked on.

'Think about it, Manny. You're gonna be sixteen this weekend, yeah? An' you wanna show them that you ain't no kid? So this is like saying, "Yo, I'm a man now and ain't nuthin' you gonna say or do, gonna stop me doin' what I want".'

Ady's *Fresh Prince* act kind of made everything a joke, but he was right. At least that's the way I thought at the time.

'Think about it, man. All free too.'

'I ain't got no money, though,' I told him. 'I'm gonna have to nick some out of one of my brothers' wallets.' I spoke really quietly, making sure that neither of my sisters-in-law could hear me.

'Fret not, dear boy. Uncle Ady has the wonga.'

'Yeah, all right then, I'll meet you up by St Philip's Church.' I'd been sold.

As soon as I said it, Ady started laughing. I swore at him and put the phone down, then turned my attention to finding Ranjit's wallet. I knew that he hadn't taken it out with him. He never did. All the money that came into the house was put together, like a

3 **to dump sb** to tell sb your relationship to them is finished – 18 **extension** room built on to a house – 36 **to fret** to worry – 36 **wonga** (*BE inf*) money

pool, and everyone that worked gave a share to cover the bills and food and stuff. I did feel bad about taking his money. I knew that it was wrong. But the way that I saw it, they were all more in the wrong than me, for making my life such a misery. I mean, all I wanted to do was be normal, like Ady and all my other friends at school. I just had a different way of going about it, that's all.

The night was wicked. There were two brilliant House DJs from Leicester playing, Bump Allen and The Baron. Neither Ady nor me really liked house music but the stuff that they played was really good. Ady seemed to know everyone in there, through his brother, and we didn't pay for a single drink in the end which was a major bonus. I was still drunk and buzzing with excitement when I climbed through my bedroom window at three in the morning. I'd been bricking it all the way home, thinking that the old man would be waiting up for me. I'd sneaked out before and not been caught, but never until that sort of time, so I was half-expecting my dad to be in my room with a bottle of Teacher's in one hand and his shoe in the other. But nobody noticed a thing. I could hardly believe it. It was like everything was going my way for a change.

Chapter Twelve
End of November

After the night out with Ady I was on full bad bwoi attack. I didn't get into school until after eleven the following day because I just couldn't get out of bed. I had a major hangover and something in my head – the rebellious bit – was telling me to stick two fingers up at the whole world. I just told Mr Sandhu that I had lost my alarm clock, then spent the whole day in a daze, not bothering to get involved in any of the lessons and spending my time doodling in the back of my folders.

On the way home I walked into the village with two of my classmates. I nicked them both a bar of chocolate from the shop which they happily took. I was buzzing. Even when I got home I was in a good mood and managed to smile at Ranjit and Jas, which gave them a bit of a shock.

'You up to something, innit?' was all that Ranjit could say.

---

12 **to buzz with excitement** [bʌz] to be elated and agitated, to look forward to something very strongly – 23 **hangover** the feeling one has the day after a night of drinking alcohol – 24 **to stick two fingers up** to raise the index and middle finger as a sign of rebellion – 26 **in a daze** unable to think clearly – 28 **to doodle** to draw something when you are bored or thinking about something else

'Nah, man. I ain't up to nothing.' My smile widened as I replied.

'Just don't let me catch you.'

'Yeah, whatever.'

I spent the whole night writing short stories in one of my A4 pads – stories about moving house and living in a beach hut in Jamaica. Fantasy stuff. I had spent so long just thinking about my ideal way of living that I had decided about a year earlier to write it all down. It was fun. Just me and my thoughts, written down in a way that no-one else but me could understand. I mean, they could read it – my family – but they'd never understand it. Then again, Harry probably wouldn't even have been able to read it, full stop! My room, with posters of Liverpool all over the walls, was like my little hidey-hole. It wasn't like before, when I had had to share with Harry and put up with the mess and the smell. It was all mine. And it was private. Being a teenager was hard enough without some privacy. I mean, once, when I had shared with Harry, I had caught him wanking while he was looking at pictures of half-naked women in *Loaded*. It was well embarrassing, especially for him.

My actual birthday was on a Saturday and, when the day came, my old man decided that I should go to the pub with him and my brothers in the evening because I was a man now – now my intended bride had been to England and the 'engagement' was all set up. It was all really macho stuff.

The pub was like an Asian-only social club on Evington Road and it was really tacky inside: tatty seats, card tables and a pool table in the corner. Bhangra music was blasting out of four ancient speakers that looked like they had been made before the war. It was full of men too – not a single woman in the place – and they were all pissed and swearing and shouting at each other. My brothers were loving every minute of it because all their mates were there. It was all 'innit' and 'wicked'. By about ten-thirty I was so bored that I told my old man I was going to get a kebab and walk home. I thought that he would tell me to wait for him but he was so pissed that he handed me a twenty-pound note and told me that he'd see me at home. I looked over at Harry, sitting with a bottle of Holsten Pils and a triple shot of neat Bacardi, then went over to tell him that I was going. He started to laugh at me.

---

18 **to wank** [wæŋk] *(inf, vul)* to masturbate – 27 **tacky** cheap and tasteless – 27 **tatty** *(inf)* in bad condition, full of holes, torn – 39 **neat** [niːt] undiluted, pure

'Look at him,' he said to his mates, pointing at me. 'Doesn't want to be a Punjabi, man. Wants to be like a *gorah*, innit. Thinks he's better than us.'

I looked around at all of his mates. They were all just like him: overweight with greasy hair, wearing gold sovereigns and black leather jackets like it was the latest fashion. Some of them had heavy gold rings in each ear and wore a gold *khanda* – the symbol of Sikhism – on a chain, around their necks but over the top of their shirts or jumpers even though they weren't real Sikhs. Real Sikhs wore turbans and didn't drink alcohol. For my brothers and their mates, it was just an image they liked to portray.

'See him, the wanker, the virgin,' Harry carried on. '*Ehnu ki patthah* (what does he know?) Thinks he's cool, innit, hanging about with *kaleh*. Wait till it all comes to a fight, innit. See if your *kaleh* friends gonna help you then.'

All his mates were laughing at me and I was getting angry. I wanted to pick up Harry's bottle of lager and smash it over his head, the fat bastard!, but I stayed as calm as I could and gave him some back.

'At least I didn't have to get married to have sex, you arsehole. And at least I have a shower every day.'

Harry's mates began to laugh at him a little and I could see that he was going red.

'All you are is an immature little mummy's boy,' I continued. 'With a body odour problem, man. Big time.'

'Shut it or I'm gonna slap you up.' Harry was getting madder and madder and I couldn't wait to turn the screw.

'I bet your wife has to wear a nose peg *and* a blindfold, you fat ugly tosser.'

That was it. The killer line. The punch. Harry shot out of his seat and grabbed me around the neck. As he did so, I threw a couple of punches at his fat belly, but they just sank into his flesh. The next thing I knew, Ranjit had pulled us apart and was walking me to the door. I looked over at my dad who was laughing at me. As I left he shouted out in Punjabi after me.

'Hey, Manjit, you're becoming a real man at last. A real Punjabi.'

I didn't bother to get a kebab or even go home. I put the twenty-pound note in my pocket and, fuming still, went to a

---

5 **sovereign** ['sɒvrɪn] (*old GB*) coin worth a pound (*here*) on a necklace – 30 **tosser** ['tɒsə] (*inf, vul*) a stupid, dislikeable person

call-box and rang Lisa who told me that it was all right to come round.

Walking to her house, a feeling started taking hold of me, as if I was being told something. About my future. I just knew, as I walked down Queens Road, that I could never fit into the kind of life that my father and brothers had. It was just too sad, too boring. I couldn't help comparing Lisa's life to mine – the way she didn't have to fight to establish herself with her family. And I'd made up my mind, by the time I reached the front door of Lisa's house, that I *was* going to break free and do my own thing. Whatever it cost...

Chapter Thirteen
December

I had to wait until lunch-time on Monday to see Lisa again. I hadn't left her house until three on the Sunday morning after talking to her and her dad about my problems. Luckily my old man and Harry had passed out by the time I got in and only Ranjit came to check on me during Sunday, just shaking his head when I told him I had got home at around one in the morning. I didn't leave my room for the whole day apart from when I went to Evington Road to get a kebab. I wasn't talking to my old man or Harry. They had really pissed me off the night before and there was no way that I was going to just forget about it. Especially not Harry – and part of my protest was not eating anything that had been made for me. Leaving the house for school on Monday morning was like being let out of prison.

Lisa came over as I was sitting on the tennis court steps watching some kids playing football.

'You all right?' she asked, kissing me on the cheek.

I looked at her and shook my head. 'I don't know. It was really nice of your dad to listen to me the other night but I still don't know what to do.'

'I really hate all this, Manny. I know it's the way your parents were brought up and the culture they live in but it makes you so sad. I wish I could change it all for you.'

8 **to establish oneself** to get a reputation and be respected in your position

'Thanks, Lisa. The way you support me and listen to me really means a lot, you know. That goes for your mum and dad too.'

'They love you, Manny – my mum's jealous that she isn't my age again!'

'I'm really glad we got together. Without you or Ady to talk to, I think I'd just go mad.'

'You're too young to have to think about so many serious things all the time.'

'I know. That's what makes me so angry all the time.' I took hold of her hand and squeezed it.

'Is that why you take so much time off school?' Lisa squeezed back.

'Yeah, in a way. I just get so pissed off, and I don't see the point of getting on well at school if it's all just a way of killing time before my parents mess up my life.'

'It's weird, I suppose,' said Lisa, before kissing me on the cheek. 'My dad and me watched this documentary about young Asian women who are forced into marriages and I always thought it was just the females that were pressured. I never realized that young men got it too.'

'I suppose it's done in a different way – like ... oh, what's the word.'

'Subliminal.'

I looked at Lisa and grinned. 'Yeah, Little Miss Dictionary. Subliminal. I mean I don't doubt that my old man would drag me to the temple if he had to. That's just what he's like. But my mum ... I mean, she hardly ever speaks to me apart from to ask me how many chapatis I want – but as soon as anyone mentions marriage and I try to say "no", the tears come out and she gets all hysterical.'

'It must be so horrible.'

'Yeah, it is. It's also upsetting and it makes me angry to a point where I just want to fight the whole world. That's when I go mad and do stupid things like go shoplifting or skive lessons to get drunk with Ady. I know it's wrong, Lisa, but I can't stop myself sometimes.'

'Well, I'm not going to pretend I like you doing those things. I think you are wrong about all that. But I *do* understand, Manny, I *really* do.'

'I know. That's why I lov...'

---

23 **subliminal** [sʌbˈlɪmɪnəl] coming from an indirect influence, something that affects you without you being aware of it *(unterschwellig)* – 28 **chapati** round flat Indian bread *(Fladenbrot)*

'See, you nearly said the dreaded L-word again,' she said referring to the number of times I'd nearly said it but, for some reason, held back. I don't think it bothered her that much. She always told me that she knew how I felt, because the way I was with her showed it so she didn't need to hear it – although I think she would have liked to. 'Look,' she continued, holding onto my thigh. 'Can you come over and stay on Saturday night?'

'Why?'

'My parents asked you to dinner, as a present for you.' She looked away and when she looked back at me she was smiling but red in the face too. 'And they want to talk to us. Both of us.'

I raised an eyebrow, wondering what she was talking about.

'I don't know what it's about, but they said it's quite important.' She looked away again.

'Dinner should be OK, but how am I going to get my old man to agree to my staying over?'

'I don't know. Can't you tell him that you'll be at Ady's house?'

'Oh yeah – the old racist is really gonna go for that.'

'Please, Manny. It's really important.' She held onto my thigh hard, looking right into my eyes. I loved the way her eyes sparkled blue-green. It always made me want to kiss her.

'I'll do my best. Honest.'

Lisa beamed at me and then kissed me and I spent the rest of the day thinking about her as I listened to my teachers droning on about Maths and Chemistry.

In the end I told Ranjit that I had a really important football trial to go to and gave him the mobile number of the teacher who was taking me and four other lads to it. Ranjit spent three or four minutes talking to our new football coach, 'Mr Menzies', the night before we were due to go and 'Mr Menzies' told him that we would be away Friday and Saturday night and that he'd personally see to my safe return on the Sunday afternoon. The trials were being held all day Saturday and Sunday morning – first at Highfield Road in Coventry, then Villa Park in Birmingham and The Hawthorns in West Bromwich on the Sunday. 'Mr Menzies' was actually Ady putting on his Merryweather and Farquar accent and at one point, when Ranjit started to go on about how it was fine with him that I went because 'footballers earn a lot of money nowadays, innit.' I had to literally bite my

---

7 **thigh** [θaɪ] front of the leg above the knee – 25 **to drone on** to talk for a long time in a boring way

own tongue to stop from laughing out loud. Ranjit even squared it with the old man and gave me twenty pounds to spend.

'You can pay me back when you sign for Man Utd, innit?' The look on his face when I went overboard with the acting and hugged him was almost complete shock. I just grinned and went to bed a happy man.

On the Friday night I went out as a foursome with Lisa, Sarah and Ady – and Ady dropped a bombshell by telling me that Sarah was pregnant and that he was looking forward to becoming a dad. I didn't know whether to laugh or cry. Ady as a father was like the biggest joke that he could ever play. I could see it all. The tiny Nike booties and baby baseball caps. The kid's first words would probably be 'Yo, man, where de honeyz at?' In the end I just shook his hand and then gave him and Sarah a hug each. What else was I supposed to do? When we got thrown out of a nightclub queue because Ady tried to blag our way in for free by insisting to the bouncers that he was Will Smith's cousin – complete with dodgy accent and all – we walked Sarah and Lisa back to Lisa's house before I went to Ady's with him and stayed over for the first time ever in our long friendship.

On Saturday I went into town with the father-to-be; I told him that we should have a look in some of the baby clothing stores, but he just played with his baseball cap and told me that he was scared stiff about it all and hadn't yet told his mum and dad. Only his brother knew and he was in no position to judge as a nineteen-year-old father of three. Later on, I bumped into Ekbal and his mates as I waited for the number 27 bus to Lisa's. He ribbed me about my 'trials', which my brothers had been bragging about, and told me that I should stand up to my old man. I said that I would call him for a chat and got on the bus feeling more than a little nervous about what Lisa's parents were going to talk to us about.

Lisa's mum let me in and kissed me on the cheek before telling me to help myself to a drink from the kitchen. Lisa was in there, standing by the fridge reading a postcard from her sister, Mel, who was travelling round Asia on a year off from uni. I kissed her hello and poured myself some orange juice from the fridge.

1 **to square sth with sb** to check with someone, to clarify things – 4 **to go overboard** to exaggerate – 8 **to drop a bombshell** to reveal big and rather shocking or unpleasant news – 16 **to blag our way in** to talk convincing nonsense in order to get in (to the nightclub) – 17 **bouncer** ['baʊnsə] *(inf)* a person e.g. hired by a nightclub to select the people that may go in and to throw the people out that cause trouble – 18 **dodgy** ['dɒdʒi] *(BE)* dubious, unconvincing – 28 **to rib** *(inf)* to tease – 29 **to brag** to show off *(angeben)*

She told me that dinner was going to be around seven, which meant that we had nearly two hours to kill.

'So, what do you want to do?' I asked, sitting down at the round kitchen table and glancing at the front page of the *Guardian*.

'I think my mum wants to talk to you before dinner,' replied Lisa.

'Yeah, but about what exactly?' Behind me Lisa's dad, who I called Ben and not Mr Jenkins, walked in and ruffled my hair.

'Hello, Manny,' he said, grabbing a glass from the cupboard and filling it with tap water. He was wearing the same kind of straight black trousers and roll-neck top that I always saw him in, with round, wire-rimmed glasses and short, trendy, messy hair which was as blond as Lisa's.

'Hi, Ben. How's it going?'

'Fine. I want to have a quiet chat with my daughter if that's all right.'

'Cool with me,' I replied.

'And I think Amanda is waiting to have a similar chat with you in the study.' He winked at me and walked out of the kitchen with Lisa following. I grabbed her hand and whispered, 'What do they want to talk about?'

She smiled and whispered back, 'Sex.'

'It's a bit of a shock really, Mrs Jenk ... Amanda.' In the study about half an hour later, I was still digesting what Lisa's mum had asked me. They knew about Ady and Sarah and, since Lisa and I were both now sixteen and had been going together a long time, they felt they needed to talk to us. Were we thinking of having sex in the near future? Were we already having sex and in that case were we using condoms? Did we realize that we had a responsibility to each other and to ourselves to make sure that we understood the physical and emotional aspects of having sex? I didn't know how to react or what to say. I just got more and more embarrassed and hoped I was saying the right thing.

And then she asked me if my parents had said anything yet. I tried to explain to her about the way I was brought up to view sex as something dirty and wrong. When I was younger my old man used to switch channels at the first sight of naked sin, even

4 **The Guardian** liberal English newspaper

on those family shows where people sent in videos of their dads mooning out of car windows and stuff. My dad would swear in Punjabi and curse white people. One night we'd been watching some Asian drama about two teenagers in Bradford. My dad had been totally engrossed until one scene in which the couple were having sex in a disused warehouse. He had hit the roof. You see, it was bad enough when he saw white people having sex on TV, but then again, he'd say, what do you expect of them? But to see Asians doing the same, especially such a pretty young Asian actress, well, that was the limit.

Amanda just gave me a hug and a kiss and told me that she was glad her daughter had such a sensitive and understanding boyfriend. Then she told me that Ben was taking her to a concert in Birmingham after dinner and that we had the house to ourselves...

Chapter Fourteen
March

That first night with Lisa really cemented our relationship and how much we loved each other. It wasn't anything like I thought it would be, our first time. It wasn't like all those scenes that you get shown by Hollywood. It was really slow and gentle and it made me realize how much she really meant to me. It sounds like something from a romance novel but there's no other way to describe it. It was amazing. We stayed up all night and talked about it and what it meant to us. I told her how glad I was to be able to spend time with her, away from my problems. When I was with her it was as if they just disappeared for a few hours and I felt relaxed and almost happy. After that night I spent a few more nights with Lisa at her parents' house, which meant that Ady got to use all of his various accents over the phone to Ranjit or his wife, Jas. The trouble was in getting back to the real world that I lived in. And there my problems just got worse.

After Christmas in Year 11, everything went downhill faster than an Olympic skier. I was skiving all the time and spending my days with Ady. Lisa was working hard for her GCSEs and I only saw her on the evenings that she had free. She continued to try and get me to attend school even though she knew by then that it was too late for me to catch up on all the work that I had missed. A couple of times I got caught – once as I was about

---

5 **engrossed** [ɪnˈgrəʊst] deeply involved, concentrating hard – 6 **to hit the roof** to be outraged

to get on the bus – and by March I was on my last chance at school. I wasn't bothered by then anyway. I hadn't really done any work for my exams and I think all the teachers had given up on me. Only Mr Cooke showed some interest, telling me that I should start working for re-sits the following year, along with an offer of private tuition if I wanted it. Lisa's dad told me much the same thing.

'You've always got an option, Manny,' he said. That was how cool Ben was. I knew that I was messing up. *He* knew it. But he just kept on telling me that I could make up for my mistakes. The only thing was, at the time, I didn't want to. My life was all about evenings spent with Lisa and her parents and sneaking out of my house to go out on the piss with Ady when he was around.

At home I hadn't really had a conversation with anyone since Christmas Day. I just got in and shut myself in my room, or I climbed out the back and went for walks up Evington Road to be on my own or to meet Ady. I was nearly at the end of five years of school, with no hope of doing well at my GCSEs and one skive away from being expelled, when Ady turned up one lunch-time. I was watching some of the other lads in my year playing football as I sat at the far end of the tennis courts having a fag.

Ady came up behind me and slapped the back of my head. I jumped to my feet and span round, fists clenched.

'Easy, rude bwoi. Wha'? You gonna beat up yuh only fren'?' He laughed as I sat back down.

'What you doin' in here? Come to do your GCSEs, man?' This time it was my turn to laugh.

Ady laughed again as he lit up a spliff that he had brought with him. 'Sack them exams, man. I got money to earn, mofo.' His accent went all gangsta-rap style.

'Well, how about sending some of that money my way?' I took the spliff as he offered it to me, blowing the smoke up into the air.

He squinted at me for a moment before replying. 'What you need money for, man? Ain't like you ever do shit anyway. Not unless I take your sad ass out.'

'I been spending loads with Lisa, man – going to the cinema and stuff.'

---

5 **re-sit** when you take an exam for a second time (because you failed the first time) – 6 **private tuition** [praɪvəttuˈɪʃən] teaching only one person, private lessons – 23 **fag** *(here, BE, inf)* cigarette – 30 **spliff** *(BE, inf)* joint, marihuana cigarette

'What you an' her still on, yeah? *How* long? Time you got yourself some fresh.'

I laughed with him. I could never get angry at Ady because everything he said was always a joke; only he could get away with it, being my best mate and everything. 'I don't want fresh, you evil drug-pusher, you. And at least I know what a condom is, *Daddy*.'

Ady winced and then ignored my jibe. 'Hey, weed is not a drug y'know.' This time the accent was broad, thick Jamaican. 'I an' I nah deal wi' dem deh drugs an' ting. Alcohol an' cigarette, dem a drug. Weed is jus' a likkle 'erb, mon.'

'Yeah, 'course it ain't a drug, and you're Bob Marley.'

Ady screwed up his face and then pulled out his pack of cigarettes. He still hadn't told me what he was doing in school.

'Well, why are you here?'

'Nice welcome, man. I come to see you, bredren, innit.' Now his voice was high-pitched and camp-sounding. It was something we did when we laughed at all the young Asian kids that talked as though they had grown up in Kingston, Jamaica, and not Rushey Mead.

'For what?'

'Well, I thought you might wanna come and have a drink or something.'

'I can't, Ady. If I get caught one more time, I'm out. For good.'

'Jus' throw a wobbly man. Tell 'em you're sick.'

'I can't, man. I'll get expelled. Not that it matters cos I'm gonna fail my exams, but the old man will go mad. School's the only escape I've got, man. Anyway why are you so keen?'

Ady looked at me and grinned cheesily. 'Because it's my birthday, bad bwoi.'

I'd forgotten. I couldn't believe it. The feeling that I got in the pit of my stomach was almost unbelievable. My best mate! My oldest and most trusted friend. And I had forgotten his birthday. Well, I mean after that, I *had* to go along with him for a drink. What else could I do?

I waited until after lunch-time to skive off. After signing in with Sandhu I went along to my art lesson. It was easy enough to

---

8 **jibe** [dʒaɪb] allusion – 8 **weed** [wiːd] *(inf)* marijuana – 10 **dem deh** "them there" *(these words are Jamaican slang and carry no meaning)* – 10 **an' ting** "and thing" *(more Jamaican slang; the words also carry no meaning)* – 11 **likkle 'erb** "little herb" – 16 **bredren** "brethren" *(Biblical / Jamaican way of saying "brothers")* – 25 **to throw a wobbly** to pretend that you are weak and not feeling well – 26 **expel** to throw a pupil out of school

get out of because the teacher, Mrs Devonshire, was really dim. She spent more time worrying about her hair and her nails than watching what the students got up to. And she always wore the same perfume, which smelled more like air-freshener than anything else. I told her that I had a bad stomach and needed the loo. She didn't even register what I said; it was that easy. The art department was round the back of the school and I had no trouble sneaking out and heading for the cover of some trees by the railings. Ady was waiting for me and we headed into Evington village.

I think that we must have sat there in the village pub for ages. I didn't really notice the time because Ady kept on buying us both double brandies with coke. We thought that we might get grief from the bar staff for being underage, but they didn't even give us a second glance, even though I was still in my uniform – without the tie, of course. I mean, it must have been obvious that we weren't old enough to be in there, but Ady must have spent thirty quid on drinks and nuts and things, and at the end of the day that was probably all the landlord and the brewery company cared about.

We talked about Sarah being pregnant and the fact that she was five months gone and Ady still didn't know what he was going to do. He told me that he felt a little bit trapped but that he wasn't blaming anyone else but himself for feeling that way.

'Man,' he said wearily, holding the peak of his cap, 'I should have seen what my brother is going through. I should have took the necessary steps an' that – it's just that when we were there and everything was cool and we was both up for it, I didn't even think about no babies. I was just being a man.'

'I dunno what to say to you, brotherman. I always use a condom.'

'Yeah, well you've got enough grief without getting some girl in trouble.' He raised his hands to the heavens and cried out 'Hai Rabbah', imitating my mother. Everyone in the pub turned to look but we just sat there laughing. After a while he went back to being serious. He scratched his forehead and then flicked his glass with a fingernail. 'Some man I was being. If I was a real man, I would have took more care – or I'd have a job now, so that I could support my girl and my kid. Shit, Manny, it even hurts to say "kid".'

'So what you gonna do?'

---

1 **dim** *(inf)* stupid – 6 **loo** *(BE, inf)* toilet – 9 **railing** metal fence – 18 **quid** *(BE inf)* pounds (money)

'What do you think? I ain't letting society stereotype me like they do with other black men. I'm gonna get a job and take care of my kid.'

By the time that I realized it was gone three o'clock, we were both hammered. I had to sneak back into school and get to my second lesson, History. It was with a supply teacher and I had planned to use the excuse that I had been in the toilets with my dodgy stomach. But I should have been there at three and I had to drag Ady out of the pub. I can't remember which one of us decided that it would be funny to sneak Ady into school too, but by the time we got back in, through the art department, I felt really sick. My head was spinning and there was no feeling in my legs. We sneaked along the corridors and up the stairs to the Humanities area without being seen by anyone apart from the old bag that worked in the school library and she was so senile that an elephant wearing a dress could have got in without her saying anything.

I walked into the classroom first and sat down, my head still spinning. I was going to be sick and I started thinking that by vomiting my story would stand up. You know, be more believable. Ady walked in about a minute after me, sat down behind me and blew my story out of the sky. The other kids watched him and started laughing and giggling to each other. The supply teacher was quite pretty – young with dark hair – but she wasn't having any of it.

'Who are you?' she asked me, as I gulped down air.

'I'm Manny, miss. I'm not feeling too well so I've been to see the school nurse. Only she wasn't there.'

To me, what I had just said sounded perfect. Only it didn't sound perfect to everyone else. The other kids started laughing even more and I started to get confused. The teacher then turned to Ady, who just sat there and smiled at her.

'And you? I suppose you were feeling ill too? So ill that you forgot your uniform this morning?'

'I'm not allowed to wear the uniform, miss.' Ady took the Chicago Bulls cap that he was wearing off his head. 'S'gainst me religion.'

At that everyone in the whole class burst into laughter. The teacher started to go all red in the face as she shouted at us all

---

5 **hammered** ['hæməd] *(BE, inf)* drunk – 14 **Humanities** subjects of study such as literature, history, art rather than science – 15 **old bag** *(vul)* old (ugly) woman – 26 **to gulp** to swallow quickly

to calm down. And then this slimy kid called Jatinder Sangha gave the game away, just as I thought me and Ady were gonna go through on the away goals rule.

'He doesn't even go to this school, miss,' he squealed, the little git.

The teacher looked at Ady and then at me. 'Right, wait here. I'm going to get Mr Sandhu.'

As she left the room Ady winked at me and got up to leave. I got up too and stumbled over to Jatinder, standing on someone's foot on the way. I was gonna punch him for being such a grass, but the feeling of sickness came over me just as I reached his desk and I puked all over his folder and into his lap. I could hear Ady laughing as the other kids got out of their chairs and went for the door. I tried to follow them but, as I got to the door, Sandhu was walking in. All I remember is shouting 'Run, Ady, run,' before I puked on my Year Head and passed out.

I came round at home in my own bed. It was dark outside and when I looked at my watch it lit up and told me that it was past ten o'clock. I couldn't remember where I had been at all – just that I had been at school with Ady and that we had been having a laugh. My head felt really heavy, like someone had hit me with a baseball bat, and my throat was dry and sore. I blinked in the dark, trying to focus my eyes on something, when the lights suddenly came on and made me feel dizzy. I squinted up at my brother, Ranjit, who was holding a brown envelope in his hand. He was smiling at me, only it wasn't a nice smile. It was a nasty, sarcastic smile. I kept on squinting at him. My head was throbbing and my throat was dry. I needed some water.

'Nice one, innit. Well done. Trying to lose our honour all by yourself, innit. Mines and Daddy-ji's. Well, you done it now. Hope you're proud at yourself.'

With that he threw the envelope at me and left. I wanted to laugh at his English but I just felt too ill. On the desk by my bed someone had left a glass of water and it took me enough strength just to reach that. I drank the whole glass and then got up slowly. I walked over to the door and bolted it on the inside. Next I got my emergency packet of fags out from behind my bed, lit one up and opened the window so that I could get rid of the ash and the smoke. I opened the letter between drags and read it.

---

12 **to puke** [pjuːk] *(inf)* to vomit – 12 **lap** the upper part of the legs when sitting *(Schoß)* – 24 **to squint** to close your eyes almost completely as a response to irritation *(blinzeln)* – 36 **to bolt** to close firmly, lock

The letter was from school, telling me that my education was done. Finished. Over. I felt sick; my stomach was turning and my head started spinning all over again. Up until that point I had been so sure of what I was doing, with the cheat and everything, to a point where I didn't care. Now I actually felt scared. I couldn't stop thinking about what I had done and whether it was right and fell asleep still thinking about it.

Chapter Fifteen
April–May

'You *will* go to India with us. I'm not asking you, Manjit, I'm telling you.'

Harry was standing in the doorway to my room holding a cup of tea. I hadn't been out of the house unsupervized since the week that I had been expelled from school. It was coming up towards May and I had been kicked out at the end of March. In all that time I hadn't seen Lisa or Ady. Ady had called me, a few weeks back, with a message from Lisa asking me to meet her in town. There had been fat chance of that though. A couple of times she had tried calling the house, but each time Harry answered and told her that I was out and then gave me loads of grief about who she was.

It was as if I was being held prisoner. Harry had been made redundant from work just before my drinking binge with Ady and now he was acting like my jailer, watching my every move, every minute of every day. On Ranjit's days off, he would take over Harry's role and at the weekends I had to deal with the pair of them *and* my old man. I was really missing Lisa and, with every day that I remained a prisoner, I became more and more depressed. I couldn't do anything. I didn't want to do anything. All my CDs began to sound the same. My gamestation got boring and I couldn't face reading my books over and over again. I got so bored that I didn't bother to get out of bed until late afternoon and then I'd be back in bed by eleven each night. All I did was eat and sleep and watch the portable TV that Ranjit's wife, Jas, had lent to me out of sympathy. She was the only one who had bothered to find out how I was. The rest of them either shouted at me and threatened me or they totally ignored me. And my mum, well, all she did was burst into tears at the mention of my name, threatening to kill herself because I had caused the

20 **to be made redundant** to get dismissed from work, to become unemployed –
21 **drinking binge** [bɪndʒ] period of hard drinking

family so much shame and because I wouldn't straighten out and become a good boy like my brothers.

And that was where the whole thing about India came in. A few years earlier one of my cousins, Parmjit, had started taking lots of drugs and burgling houses and stuff. He had been sent to a youth detention centre for eight months and, the moment he was released, my uncle had forced him to go to India. He had made him stay in my family's village for nearly a whole year, to try and 'straighten him out' as my dad had put it. Make a real Punjabi man of him. And it had worked. He had married some girl from a neighbouring village and come back to England a changed person. Now he had a family and a mortgage and a dead-end job in a factory – and he was only twenty-one. That was what my old man was dreaming would happen to me.

I knew that I was too strong for that. That wasn't how I wanted my life to be. I didn't want a wife and a mortgage. Didn't want to be an average bod. That wasn't the future for me. No way. And I'd been telling them that since the day after I had been expelled – not that they listened.

Harry kept on telling me that he was going to force me to go. My dad just laughed when I said no, mocking me like I was some four-year-old child having a sulk. And my mum just kept on crying, begging them to make me see the light and calling out to God. It was emotional blackmail at its worst, all of her moaning and wailing and that, but it was the only one of my family's tactics that made me think about it. See, no matter how sure I was that my mother wouldn't really kill herself because of me, I still had all of these doubts that said she just might.

'I ain't going nowhere. Why should I?'

Harry looked at me angrily. He shifted from foot to foot. I thought that I could almost hear his teeth grinding together. 'You ain't going to be the cause of shame to this family, you little bastard. The whole decision's been taken, innit. You going to go even if I have to beat you to make you go.'

I looked at him and shook my head. I wanted to make a run for it. Just bolt out of the door and down the stairs. But where was I going to go? What was I going to do? Where was the money for food and all of those things going to come from? I wasn't just physically trapped by then, I was trapped because I was

6 **youth detention centre** a prison for adolescents – 12 **mortgage** ['mɔːɡɪdʒ] loan, money from the bank *(Hypothek)* – 17 **bod** *(BE)* person – 22 **to have a sulk** [sʌlk] to be quiet but obviously in a bad mood *(schmollen)* – 25 **to wail** [weɪl] to lament, to moan – 31 **to grind** [ɡraɪnd] the noise made when sth is crushed to powder – 36 **to bolt** [bəʊlt] to run off

so young. I mean, I couldn't get benefits and I didn't have the qualifications to get a job, even if my family would let me. I really *was* stuck with the situation that I was in. Well and truly.

'You understand what I'm saying, Manjit?'

I looked up at him again and smiled. It must have been an annoying smile because Harry just stood there and glared. I looked away and lay back on my bed.

'You better understand, innit, or I'll kick you in. It's simple, innit. You're coming to India and that's all I'm gonna say.'

With that he turned and walked out of my room, leaving the door open behind him. I got off my bed in a fit of rage and kicked the door shut so hard that I thought the door-frame was going to fall apart. It didn't, but small flakes of white paint came away from the edges of the door, leaving the undercoat showing through. Normally I would have bricked myself for causing such damage but I wasn't in the mood to be scared. I was far too angry with all of them.

In my head something was thumping, stabbing. It was as if my brain was being taken apart. I just stood where I was, looking at the damaged paintwork and I couldn't think straight. I couldn't work out what to do or what I wanted to say. All I knew was that I felt totally alone. I had always believed that I was different from the rest of my family. Not better than them or anything like that. Just *different*. But it was in my room, staring at that door, trying to think straight, that it really hit me. I *was* different. Completely. And I had to find a way out. Work out how I was going to get out of this marriage, get away from them for good. I sat back on my bed and, not for the first time, thought hard. Really hard.

After all that, I suppose you're wondering why I relented and decided to make the trip to India with my family. After all, it was a big climb-down on my part – a bit like Liverpool conceding the Premiership to Moneybags United by March. In the end it was the combination of all the emotional blackmail that I had to put up with and a change in tactics by my family. My dad started being really nice to me, telling me that it was my decision at the end of the day but that it wouldn't kill my mother if I didn't go with them to India. It was only a holiday, a chance for the family to spend some time together. And it wasn't as if I had a job or would be going back to school again. And my wedding wasn't until the late summer – or maybe even a month or so

---

1 **benefits** ['benɪfɪts] money from the government e.g. when unemployed – 6 **to glare** [gleə] to look angrily

later. So why not take a holiday now? He began to make me feel that it would be down to me to decide, and to tell you the truth, that felt good. It felt like my family, for the first time ever, were taking my views seriously. Treating me like the adult that I was becoming.

One evening, I think it was in late May, Ranjit's wife, Jas, knocked on my bedroom door. I did what I always did and kind of grunted at her, my way of saying 'Come in'.

She walked in and sat down on my bed, smiling. 'How are you, Manny?'

'All right, I suppose.' I was busy staring at a blank screen on my TV, the one that she had given to me. I didn't mind her too much because she never shouted at me or anything. She had always been a little bit embarrassed by the rest of my family's attitude towards me, or that's how it seemed. As I watched the blank screen she began talking to me, asking me how I felt and telling me that she realized that being stuck at home all the time was hard for me.

'You must miss your friends from school.'

I nodded, thinking of Lisa. I hadn't seen her for so long. I was missing her badly and I'm sure that if Jas hadn't been sitting there, I would have cried. Every time I thought about Lisa, my stomach just turned over and I got depressed which, in turn, made me feel angry towards my family.

I was missing Ady too, although in a different way. Even at school I had been used to not seeing him for weeks on end and it didn't seem so bad now – didn't feel as bad as it felt not seeing Lisa. I had to take a big swallow of air before I could look at Jas.

'This trip to India,' she began, 'this holiday, Manny. That's all it is, honestly.'

I heard her but I wasn't really listening to what she said. I was listening to the way that she spoke English. It was normal, good even. I wondered whether she had GCSEs. It was weird. Jas had been part of the family for so long and I really didn't know anything about her at all.

'I think that it would do you good to come along. Just think of all the fun you'd have. You'd be able to go where you wanted, do what you liked.'

'What about all the crap?' I was looking straight at her now. 'All that stuff about leaving me there and making me turn into a good little boy.' My voice was thick with sarcasm.

8 **to grunt** to make a low rough sound deep in your throat

'Come on, Manny, you're an intelligent young man. How can anyone keep you there against your will?'

'That's what they've been saying, Dad and Ranjit. Telling me that I need straightening out.'

'Well, I'm promising you, that isn't going to happen.'

I looked straight into her eyes, hoping to see some kind of lie there. She was being totally genuine though. She didn't even blink.

'You're promising?'

'Yes. I promise that you won't have to stay there. We're going for eight weeks. That's all.'

I thought about it for a minute before replying. I mean, I wasn't going to come out and say 'yes' just because Jas was being nice to me. I wasn't that stupid. But deep inside I really felt that she was being truthful and, of course, she was right. How *could* they make me stay in India against my will? I wasn't a kid any more. And the way that Jas was taking an interest in me, asking me how I felt, made me feel wanted. Warm on the inside. Almost like I was a member of the family. Almost.

'I'll think about it,' I finally replied, smiling for the first time in months.

'Good. In that case you can come shopping with me. We need to buy clothes and things for the trip.'

Lisa's letter arrived about two or three days after my conversation with Jas. I had just been to the corner shop and bought myself some cigarettes. In all the time that I had been stuck at home, going to the shop for fags was about the only freedom that I got – not that my family knew I was going to buy fags, as far as I knew anyway. It was early in the afternoon and I was approaching the front gate of our driveway when I saw the postman.

'These are for you, mate,' he said handing me three envelopes.

The first was a brown envelope that looked like something official. A bill or something, for Ranjit. The second was a blue airmail envelope, addressed to my dad in scrawling handwriting. I looked at the sender's name, realizing that it was from one of my uncles in India. The third one was mine. It was a bright-red envelope with my name on it, and the handwriting was definitely Lisa's. My heart jumped and I tucked it into the back pocket of my jeans.

Back in my bedroom I tore it open and unfolded the two sheets of red paper inside. As I began to read my mind was racing. The letter began with questions about how I was and what was going on. Why hadn't I met her in town? Why wasn't I going to another school? She wrote that she really missed me and was always asking Sarah and Ady about me. She also told me that her parents were worried about me too and wanted to know if they could help me in any way. Then she hit me. Hard.

... I don't know what to do about this whole situation, Manny. What do I do? I mean we haven't seen each other for so long and I don't think we will, will we? Not for a long while. So I've decided to go to Australia for the summer to meet up with Mel. I really don't know what is happening between us. I know that I love you but I can't just not see you. It just doesn't work. What do you think? I'm sorry if you're upset but you have to see it from my point of view. I don't even know if I will see you again. Or whether you'll be married by the time I get back in September. I don't want to do this, Manny, but I have to otherwise I'll go mad. Please sort things out – for you and for us. Oh, I feel so selfish in writing this. I'm so sorry.

e-mail me if you can. I've put Mel's address at the bottom of the page. And if you decide to leave, to get away, my mum and dad say that you can move in with them for a while. Please think about it. Please. I'll really miss you...

I didn't bother to finish it because I was too upset. It felt as though she was dropping me, after everything that we had said to each other about wanting to be together. My brain was going in all sorts of different directions and I didn't have a clue what to think or what to do. I got up, shut my bedroom door and put my stereo on. Then I sat down and cried.

I didn't leave my room until half-seven that night. I went down into the kitchen to get a drink because my mouth was feeling dry. Jas was in there making chapatis for the evening meal. She smiled as I walked in.

'Do you want some roti?'

I watched my nephew, Gurpal, as he toddled around the kitchen. 'No,' I replied, pouring myself a glass of Coke. 'Ain't hungry. I might make a sandwich later.'

'You're sure?'

'Yeah. Jas, you know what you said about India...?'

'What about it, Manny?' She was staring at me now, wiping flour from her hands onto a tea towel.

'I'll go. But only if you can still promise what you said the other day.'

'I promise.'

She came over and hugged me. I had to stop myself from crying again, but I didn't cry. Not in front of her. Not in front of anyone. I just went back upstairs to my room, played some more music, chilled out and thought about what I was going to do with my life. Without Ady. Without Lisa.

part three

india

Chapter Sixteen
June

The first thing that struck me when we got off the Air India plane at Delhi airport was the heat. It was five to two in the morning and the temperature must have been about thirty degrees. I was wearing a pair of jeans, trainers, a T-shirt and hooded top and almost straight away I wanted to take everything off. We hadn't even reached the customs area before the sweat was streaming down my face and my legs started to ache. I looked at Harry and wondered how he was going to smell after our first hour in India.

The queues were already quite long at the checkpoint booths and I watched as the people in front of us showed their passports and answered the guards' questions. It was only when we got to within three people of the front that I realized that they were wearing gun holsters and had rifles standing next to their stools in the booths. I was wondering why they needed guns at an airport when my dad pulled me alongside him and motioned for me to show the guard my ticket and passport. The guard was really dark and had oily hair that was parted to the left. I smiled at him as he compared my face to the photo in my passport but he just glared back at me, expressionlessly. Then he motioned with his head for us to go through into the arrivals area. As I walked through the gate I couldn't take my eyes off the gun that was leaning against his stool.

The arrivals area was also patrolled by armed guards in green army outfits and as we made our way out towards the exit doors of the airport building, they kept on glaring and watching everything that we did. Harry and Ranjit had gone to get our suitcases and bags so I waited near the doors with Jas, Gurpal and Harry's wife, Baljit. My mum and dad were standing further into the airport talking to a couple who they had met on the plane. They were from the village next to my father's and were going to travel to the Punjab with us.

Harry came back first, pushing a trolley. Sitting on the top was my black backpack which I pulled off and then hung from my shoulder. Inside it was my personal stereo and four packets of Benson & Hedges which I had hidden underneath some paperback books and a copy of *Loaded*. The bag also contained an A4 writing pad and a set of four smaller notebooks that would fit into my back pocket. It was my boredom survival kit,

6 **customs** the place at an airport or port where your luggage is checked (*Zoll*)

my escape route back into the world that we had left behind after flying for nearly ten straight hours. You see, I was looking forward to being in India, to seeing how different it was from England, and at the same time I didn't want to be in India when I could be in Leicester. I was excited about the travelling because I had always dreamed about going to new places and doing new things, but not with my family in tow. In my daydreams I would travel the world with Ady or with Lisa, or one of my other friends. Sometimes I'd even travel alone. Those were always the best daydreams. Not in any one of those dreams would I be travelling with Harry or Ranjit, or cringing with the shame of hearing my mum shouting at the top of her voice in Punjabi across the crowded check-in lounge at Heathrow.

I wanted a cigarette really badly and I looked up and down the main foyer of the airport building, looking for the toilets. Then I told Harry where I was going and he grinned like an idiot.

'Going for a fag, I bet.'

I smiled back at him, kind of sarcastically, before heading off. I walked straight into one of the cubicles and locked the door before rummaging around in my bag for my cigarettes. The smoke was like sandpaper as it entered my dry mouth and I realized that I also needed a drink. Badly. At least the sweat had stopped streaming down my face. I pulled the toilet lid down and sat, trying to work out how I was going to get Indian money from my old man to buy more fags with and where exactly I was going to buy them from.

Outside the airport we made our way towards the main bus station. It didn't matter where you wanted to go in India; once you got off the plane at Delhi airport, the next part of your journey started at that bus station. The air outside was really dry and the smell of diesel was all around us. Everywhere I looked I could see people milling around, some of them travellers, but mostly beggars. They searched my face as I walked by, holding out their hands. There were men, women, old people and toddlers. And they were everywhere. All of them wearing rags – if they wore anything at all – and none of them wearing any shoes. I was kind of shocked by it all. I had seen homeless people begging in Leicester before but only ever a few at a time. Here I was in the country that my old man was always calling the best in the world and there were hundreds of them. If I had

---

11 **to cringe** [krɪndʒ] to feel very embarrassed or ashamed – 19 **cubicle** [ˈkjuːbɪkl] small room, *here* section of the toilet *(Kabine)* – 20 **to rummage around** to look for (in a random way) – 32 **to mill around** to wander around aimlessly – 37 **rags** torn material clothes *(Fetzen)*

been carrying any money, I'm sure that I would have given it all away. I mean, some of the naked kids were just babies, maybe two or three years old, and I was beginning to feel really sorry for them and guilty about being so rich in comparison. My own
5 nephew was about that sort of age himself and I wondered how I'd feel if he was put in the same situation. I was having all these well heavy, deep thoughts looking at all the beggars and I'd only been in the country an hour.

We caught a battered old bus to somewhere called Kashmiri
10 Gate where, according to my father, we'd be able to get a coach for Jullundur which was the main city in Nawanshar, the area where my father's village was. The bus had all the glass from the windows missing and the seats were just wooden slats screwed onto metal posts that stuck out of the floor. Every minute or so
15 the wheels hit potholes or rode over things that had been left on the road, and the bus jolted around really badly.

The road was in total chaos. There were animals walking around and people who just wandered in groups, across the path of the bus. I saw a motorcycle, crushed in some kind of
20 accident, that had just been left in the road and every time another vehicle rumbled past I was convinced that we would hit it. Some of the huge trucks that went by every few minutes came so close to my face, I thought I was going to get pulled out of the bus by the rush of air. It was a nightmare.

25 It was a nightmare that got worse. At Kashmiri Gate we couldn't find the right stand for our coach and the drivers just wandered about, not bothering to answer anyone's questions. I asked Ranjit why we didn't just find the ticket office and he laughed at me.

30 'You stupid, guy, or what? They ain't got ticket offices here. You just pay the driver, innit.'

I looked at him, not knowing what to say. I felt as if I was almost in shock. There were loads of buses and coaches and around each stand there were hundreds of people, all pushing
35 and shoving each other, whilst in amongst all of the travellers, hundreds more homeless people begged for money. It was mad. Ranjit pointed to a stand at the far end of the open courtyard which made up the station. The old man was standing by it talking to a huge bloke in a red turban. They talked for a bit
40 and then my dad handed over some money. Ranjit grabbed me

11 **Jullundur** ancient city, third largest city in Punjab – 11 **Nawanshar** Punjabi district – 13 **slat** a narrow strip of wood – 15 **pothole** ['pɒthəʊl] a large hole in the road which makes a journey uncomfortable – 37 **courtyard** area of flat ground surrounded by buildings *(Hof)*

and told me to follow him. Jas, holding Gurpal, my mum and
Baljit were already walking over to where my dad was standing.
I couldn't see Harry. Just for a moment I hoped that we had lost
him back at the airport, only to feel his hand on my shoulder,
and his mouth near my ear.

'Watch your bag man. These *chamarr* (low castes) will rob
anything. Best the government should just round them up and
kill 'em, innit.' I was so disgusted at what he said that my head
started to shake, of its own accord. Harry just grinned at me – a
big, stupid, fascist ape.

The 'coach' turned out to be the twin of the bus that we had
taken from the airport, only this one still had a few pieces of
glass in some of its windows. The driver was a Punjabi man who
had agreed to take us to the Punjab for a price. Jas told me that
he was a private hire driver who was supposed to be on his way
home for the night. My dad had offered him money to hire his
'coach' and he had agreed even though he looked like he had
just finished a long day. He produced a couple of cushions to
make my mum's ride more comfortable, but all I got was more
wooden slats. I suppose it was good that the only other people
on the bus were the couple from the airport, but I was annoyed
at the state of it. My dad had been promising me all the way
from Leicester that we would travel on a luxury coach. The only
luxury I could find was a seat next to another window missing
glass and a whole piece of wood to myself, although by then
I had wised up and was using my top as a cushion. At least it
couldn't be that far to the Punjab, I told myself. Wanting to make
sure, I turned around to Ranjit, who was sitting behind me, with
Gurpal sleeping on his lap, and asked him.

'Not long, innit,' he grinned. ''bout six, seven hours. Maybe
eight.'

He started laughing as he saw the look on my face. *Eight hours!*
How was I going to put up with that? I turned to look out of my
window and watched the same chaos that I'd seen on the road
from the airport to the bus station over every road all the way
through Delhi – past roundabouts covered in sleeping homeless
people, grass verges with bulls and pigs roaming wild on them,
and over what felt like a pothole every ten seconds. Once out
of Delhi the road was in total darkness, the only light coming
from the headlights at the front of the bus. Every few miles a
huge truck sped past us, appearing out of nowhere, with neither
the bus driver or the truck drivers giving an inch. There didn't

36 **roundabout** construction which divides two perpendicular roads *(Kreisverkehr)* –
37 **verge** [vɜ :dʒ] *(here)* grass strip

seem to be any rules on the road about which side to drive on, or staying in lane, speed limits. Nothing. Realizing that I wasn't going to be able to sleep, not comfortably anyway, made me feel even more miserable. The only person asleep was my nephew and he could sleep through anything. I suppose it wouldn't be a lie for me to say that I spent the entire journey bricking myself every time another bus or truck passed us, convinced that I was going to die. By the time it began to get light I was all bleary-eyed and in a daze. I was hot, smelly, tired, thirsty. Dying to close my eyes and just sleep. Like, for a month.

We made it to Jullundur at just gone one in the afternoon and the sun was beating down, melting the cheap tarmac used on the roads. I had never felt heat like it. Ever. If you took the hottest day that you'd ever seen in England and added ten degrees, you'd be close to feeling the kind of heat that I was feeling. I couldn't even sweat any more because the last drinks we had stopped for had been about four hours earlier, and the fluid from them was already well out of my system. The local people at Jullundur just milled about like it was nothing. I would have given up my new Air Max for a can of Coke straight from the fridge. We got off the bus in the centre of the city and my dad went off to find a taxi, leaving us all standing in the heat by the roadside.

We stood around for about half an hour or so before the taxi turned up. My dad had hired it to take us to the village which was about half an hour's drive from the city according to my mum. The taxi itself was an old Ambassador, like a 1930s American gangster's car although not as old as that. It was a pretty big car but I couldn't see how all of us would fit in it. I mean, with all of us and the other couple, there were eight adults, one almost adult – me – and a toddler who seemed the most comfortable of all of us in our strange surroundings. Somehow the driver managed to get all of our luggage into the big boot at the back, apart from a couple of the bigger suitcases, which he tied to a rusty-looking roof rack. In the front of the car there was only one continuous seat and my father shared that with Harry, the man from the next village and the driver. I got to sit in the back, squashed against the passenger side door, next to Ranjit, whilst Baljit, who was really thin anyway, was virtually sitting in Jas's lap along with Ranjit's son, Gurpal. And next to them the two old dears. Squashed up like sardines in a can, we began the final stretch of our journey to the village where my father had grown up – Adumpur.

8 **bleary-eyed** ['blɪəriːˈaɪd] having red and watery eyes due to being very tired – 12 **tarmac** asphalt

Chapter Seventeen
June

As we approached Adumpur, I began to take a look at the landscape. I noticed that the village was surrounded on all sides by really flat land. For miles in each direction there were only fields and the occasional village. The first houses that I saw were square, box shapes and none of them had a roof. They were all shabby-looking and coloured off-white. A group of about five houses lined the right side of the dirt track that passed for a road; to the left there was a huge lake, in which a herd of water buffalo were standing. It couldn't have been very deep because some of the animals were almost standing in the middle of it, and floating on its surface there was some kind of scum. The water looked horrible, all dark and murky. I saw two young kids, probably only two or three years younger than me, watching the herd. One of them, tall and skinny, held a long stick in his hands which he used to guide the water buffalo.

The taxi moved slowly through the village, along streets which in places were so narrow that the taxi was the only thing that could pass. The house fronts were all painted in pastel shades – pinks and blues and yellows – and the windows had steel bars, netting and shutters. Almost every other house had hanging baskets of flowers above the windows and suspended over the doors. These houses were only two storeys high and my dad told me that they were like townhouses; most of the richer families, including ours, had houses out in the fields too, built around wells. Farmhouses. I was getting impatient. I wanted to see our house now, compare it to the ones that I had seen so far. The old man told me that our house was on the other side of the village, past the central square and the shops. The 'shops' turned out to be open-fronted huts and there were only three of them. Without getting out of the taxi, I couldn't tell you what they sold, although I did notice a fading cigarette advert posted by the side of one of them. I made a mental note to explore the area when I got the chance.

Past the centre of the village the streets widened and we passed a gurudwara that was painted in brilliant white and decorated with outside lights, like a Christmas tree. Its huge front doors were wide open and inside it looked rather ornate, not like the ones in England. The temple stood on its own and the next house

---

11 **scum** film of dirty matter which forms on the surface of water – 20 **netting** net, mesh – 20 **shutters** wooden or metal covers to shut out the light of a window – 21 **to suspend** *(here)* to hang – 37 **ornate** [ɔːˈneɪt] elaborately decorated

that we came to was massive. It must have taken up the same amount of space as five or six of the smaller townhouses that we had passed earlier. The house was set back from the street, a wall about three metres high running right around it, with two iron gates at the front. Behind the wall was a garden and a really English-looking driveway. There were two cars standing on the drive, one a Jeep and the other a Mercedes lookalike that Ranjit said was a Tata. The house itself was four storeys high and each upper storey had a balcony that seemed to run right around each floor. The ground floor had a glass-fronted veranda and through the glass I could see plants and hanging baskets. At the very top of the house were turrets and at the front, in the very middle, there was Punjabi writing on a plaque.

'What does that say, Daddy-ji?' I asked in my best Punjabi. 'That sign?'

'It spells out the name of their family, Manjit. Letting everyone that sees it know how well they have done for themselves.'

'Which family, ours?'

'No, it is another family. They own factories in Birmingham. Make plenty of money, and I tell you, not one of them went to university and bloody college.'

I looked at the house as we passed it by and then back at my dad.

Ranjit pointed at the house, smirking. 'What's this anyway? We are going to build a better house than this when we get the chance. Isn't that right, Daddy-ji?' Ranjit's Punjabi was a lot better than mine although I knew that mine would improve. After all, that was all I was going to be speaking for the next two months.

My dad just sighed and put his hands together in prayer. 'Only if God wills it,' he replied. And then quickly added, 'And my sons wish to honour my name.' He looked at me. I returned his look and then turned my head to carry on staring out of the window.

My father's childhood home wasn't quite the place that he had been describing, continually, on the plane journey from England. I had imagined it painted in a bright colour, with guava trees growing in the courtyard and maybe a couple of mango trees. Climbing plants and flowers would be growing across the walls with hanging baskets crowded with wicked colours. A tractor, gleaming bright-red, would be in the yard and there would be pets running around with colourfully dressed kids

24 **to smirk** [smɜːk] to smile in an unpleasant, self-satisfied way – 37 **guava** tropical fruit with pink flesh and a lot of seeds

chasing them. All the wonderful things that my dad used to tell us about it as kids.

A two-storey building with an open rooftop and a courtyard at the front, the house had obviously been wonderful and colourful once. But now it was painted a shade of pastel pink in a mixture of whitewash and colouring. It looked as though it hadn't seen a new coat for a few years. Here and there the paint was flaking from the walls and in a few places cracks had appeared, running the whole length, from ceiling to floor, or the other way round as I was told later. I couldn't tell the difference myself. The gates into the courtyard from the street were rusted and looked in need of new hinges as they scraped across the floor to let us through. In the courtyard the first things that I noticed were the water buffalo tied against a wall in the farthest corner from the house. There were three females and two young calves. One of the females was pregnant, my dad told me, the biggest one. Again I couldn't tell the difference because they all looked massive to me. There was a trough of water alongside the water buffalo and sitting on top of it was a little kid dressed only in shorts. He must have been about five or six and, even though he was really skinny, already he had more muscle definition across his stomach and chest than I had. I was almost jealous. He smiled and waved at us as we walked in and I kind of nodded back at him, wondering who he was.

The floor of the courtyard was covered in about a centimetre of dust and dirt and it crunched under the soles of my Air Max. Opposite the buffalo were two or three sheds. Only one of them had a door and it sat open with what looked like bales of hay falling out. Running across the yard, in front of the house, was a low wall painted the same shade as the house, with a gate in the middle. At various points along the wall there were little shrubs planted in the dirt and, in each corner, a guava tree. Diamond-shaped holes formed a pattern across the width of the wall.

As we walked across the courtyard towards the house a man came out to greet us. He was wearing a light-blue open-necked shirt and matching drawstring bottoms – a *kortha*, the traditional outfit of Punjabi males. On his feet he wore brown sandals without socks and his hair was shaved in what looked like a number two, close to his head. I couldn't stop staring at

---

12 **hinge** [hɪndʒ] metal part holding a door or window in its frame – 18 **trough** [trɒf] long narrow box which holds food for farm animals – 31 **shrub** small bush – 36 **drawstring bottoms** trousers with a string that you can pull to make them tighter

him. Apart from the neatly trimmed moustache and beard, he was the twin of my old man, although younger and not so fat around the waist. My dad walked over and hugged him before calling me over.

'Manjit, say hello to your Uncle Piara.'

I looked at him and smiled, replying in my best Punjabi. He smiled back and hugged me.

'At last I get to meet you too,' he said. He had met my brothers and sisters on previous visits to India, before I was born. 'Come on, Manjit,' he continued. 'You'll dry up out there.'

* * *

We spent the rest of the afternoon relaxing in the house, resting after our long journey. The inside of the house wasn't what I had been expecting either. The rooms that I saw, all of those downstairs, were pretty basic. The floors were covered in stone tiles and the walls were painted in a light-blue colour. There were no sofas or armchairs, nothing like that. No pictures hung on the walls or shelves loaded with photo frames. I couldn't even see a TV or hi-fi and realized that my decision to bring a Walkman had been a good one. We sat down on *manjeh*, which are like traditional beds and seats rolled into one. They had wooden frames which were about the length and width of my single bed at home. Around each frame were strands of rope that criss-crossed each other and were tied in each corner. These strands, woven together, made up the 'mattresses'. The weave on them looked like the stitching on those dodgy cable knit sweaters that all old Asian men seemed to wear in England, although the manjeh were actually quite comfortable to sit on. It was only slightly cooler inside the house and on each ceiling there were fans that made a whirring sound and moved warm air around the rooms. I was sat next to my Uncle Piara, feeling myself sweat really badly. When I complained my dad laughed and told me that he'd show me where the shower was soon. I was dying for a cold drink when the first of my cousins, a skinny boy called Inderjit, appeared with bottles of cola so cold that my throat started to ache as I drank it down.

The shutters across each window were pulled tight to stop the sunlight from getting in although every now and then flies would buzz through the tiny gaps that the shutters left. I

---

22 **strand** thread – 25 **dodgy** ill-fitting, tasteless – 25 **cable knit sweater** pullover with a raised pattern of crossing lines on it

guessed that the flies were like bluebottles or horseflies, only they were massive and the noise they made sounded to me like a swarm of wasps.

'They are nothing, man,' laughed Harry. 'Wait till you see the wasps, innit. They're massive, guy. Good two inches long and that.'

My uncle asked the old man why we were speaking in English and he began one of his lectures about us all thinking we were English now. If only he had stayed here, he told my uncle, they'd be good Punjabi men by now. I watched my uncle's reaction, hoping that he might disagree with the old man, but all he did was laugh at what he had said and nod his head.

'They ain't gonna be two inches long, Harry. You're just exaggerating.' I decided that I would continue speaking in English, just to get on their nerves.

''Course they are. You ain't seen them before. Two inches long.'

'Yeah, like you're kn...' I began, before Jas cut me off.

'Stop it you two, we aren't at home now. This is supposed to be a holiday.'

'Yeah,' piped up Ranjit, 'you two better cool it or I'll deal with you.'

Harry went off to join Baljit in the room next door and, just after he had left, a flying insect about an inch and a half long buzzed in through the screen door that he had left open. Its body was in two sections, coloured bright green and orange, and it had a tail which curved into a stinging point, about another half an inch. A two-inch wasp.

'Least now you know he weren't telling lies, innit,' laughed Ranjit as he removed his shoe. 'Don't worry, I'll get the little *chamarr*.'

By about six in the evening the whole family was back at the house and the light had begun to fade into dusk. I couldn't believe how quickly the darkness was coming on. It was changing right in front of my eyes. The manjeh had been taken out onto the open veranda that ran along the front of the house, separating it from the courtyard beyond. It was lovely and warm, not hot like it had been in the day, but really comfortable with a light breeze coming in across the courtyard. Above our heads three powerful bulbs lit up the area, attracting huge moths that made the sparrows in England look puny. Man, they were big and

---

1 **bluebottle** a kind of fly *(Schmeißfliege)* – 33 **dusk** the time in the evening when it gets dark – 41 **sparrow** a common bird *(Spatz)* – 41 **puny** small and weak

hairy. A bit like Harry, really. Most of the family were gathered around the veranda, the older males drinking beer and whisky and talking about boring stuff like the price of land.

The women, including my mum, were gathered around an open kitchen area at one end of the veranda, next to the entrance to an indoor kitchen. They had started an open, barbecue-style fire and were beginning to cook in pots that were so old they were burnt and blackened. The air was full of the smell of frying onions and garam masala, coriander and cardamoms. Earlier in the day my uncle had butchered a couple of chickens and filleted them. Jas, wanting to make a good impression by the look of things, told everyone about how English people had gone crazy over balti dishes, only for my uncle to suggest that she made one. I wasn't even sure that I was going to eat it, not when the chickens had been killed specially for that purpose. The shock of being so close to the actual butchering had made me feel bad.

'Don't worry,' laughed Harry. 'We'll soon make a real man of you, innit. Just wait, you *chamarr*.'

I looked around to make sure that no-one old was watching and then gave him the finger. Tosser.

My family were of the 'Jat' caste – the farmers of the Punjab – and like most other Jat families they hired a family of *Chamarr*, a lower servant-caste. I didn't really feel comfortable with the fact that we had servants because of everything I had learned from Mr Cooke at school with Ady about slavery and indentured workers. I didn't think that it was right that they were seen as lower than us simply because of who their parents were. It was just another one of those crappy ancient traditions. This particular family had apparently worked for our family for nearly three generations.

The mother of the servant family, Naseebo, usually made all the meals, and she looked a little bit lost when Jas took over the cooking. She sat and helped Jas, handing her the spices and chopping onions and garlic, but I could tell that she was a little bit put out by it. I think Jas noticed too, because she tried to make up for it by asking Naseebo and her family to stay for the meal, only to be told by my Aunt Pritam, that they always did that anyway. Jas went a bit red over Aunt Pritam's remark and for about five minutes there was a strange silence that took hold. Even the men stopped talking. Finally Uncle Piara called me

9 **garam masala** mixture of hot spices – 13 **balti** hot, curry style dish – 27 **indentured worker** worker that has officially agreed to work for someone else, often to learn a job – 36 **put out** annoyed

over to him and that got everyone going again. He handed me a bottle of beer called Cobra, and told me to have a drink. I looked at my old man who just nodded at me and then spoke up.

'Drink it, drink it. You are a man now, Manjit, not a boy. There's no problem.'

'You can't sit with the women all night, they'll send you crazy,' laughed Uncle Piara.

As I took a little swig of the bitter-tasting beer, my cousins watched me, before two of the youngest ones who were about my age – Inderjit and Jasbir – asked Uncle Piara if they could have some too. He looked at them for ages before my old man replied for him.

'You too,' he said, laughing. 'Go on. Piara won't say anything. I'm the elder here.'

At that all of them burst into laughter, leaving me trying to work out what had been so funny.

The speed of the Punjabi they were speaking in left me behind. Every so often I'd have to ask them to repeat something or say it more slowly. Occasionally I missed what they said altogether but I didn't mind. I simply sat back on the manjah and drank my beer while everyone else talked, wondering for the first time since leaving England what Ady would be up to. Then, as the breeze picked up and the beer began to go to my head, I thought about Lisa and suddenly started feeling depressed. Alone and lonely, on a veranda surrounded by my family.

Chapter Eighteen
July

Over the following couple of weeks I slowly got to know all the members of my family. The oldest person was my old man's aunt, my great aunt, who was close to being a hundred years old and looked like a bag full of bones. She was completely blind and heard very little so my Aunt Pritam took care of her. My grandparents were both dead and my great aunt was the only real elder left. Uncle Piara was married to Aunt Pritam and they had three sons and a daughter. Rana, the oldest son, was twenty-four and had been married for a few years. His wife was called Sukbir and they had two young sons, Ranjit and Harjit.

8 **swig** mouthful

After Rana came Jaspal, the only girl, who was twenty-two and married to a man called Jasbir. They had no children yet and lived in his parents' village, which was twenty miles north of Adumpur. Lal, the next son, was nineteen and had been married for about a year. His wife, Rajvir, was heavily pregnant, although, as Jas told me, it was not acceptable to mention it in front of the family. I just laughed at her. I mean they all did it, and babies were born and that, but it was all kind of hush-hush. The youngest of Uncle Piara's kids was Inderjit, who at sixteen was the same age as me. He was quite a laugh, Inderjit, and had promised to take me on a tour of the village.

After Piara came Uncle Gurvinder, who was married to Aunt Harpal. They also had four kids, three sons and a daughter, just like Uncle Piara. The oldest son was Avtar, who was twenty-two and married to a girl called Jaswant. They had three kids, two girls called Sukhjit and Manpreet, and a baby son, Gurpreet. Next came Jagwant, the only daughter, who was a year younger than Avtar and also married, to Parmjit. Neither she nor her husband had visited us yet and I didn't really know much about her at all. After her, there was Onkar, who at eighteen, had only recently got married to a girl called Balbir. And finally there was Jasbir, who at fifteen was the youngest.

Taking it all in was very confusing because all my new-found cousins and their husbands and wives had to be added to the cousins that I had back in England, the children of my old man's two eldest brothers, not to mention the youngest of my father's brothers, Jag, who was like the black sheep of the family and wasn't mentioned much. And that was before you considered my mum's side of the family which was even bigger, according to Harry. It was no surprise for me to find uncles, aunts, cousins, nieces and nephews with the same or similar names. Man, my family must have started running out of them by now. There were a few Jases, lots of Jits; even Rana, whose real name was Ranjit, had called one of his kids after himself and my oldest brother. I got used to it quite quickly though, in the same way that I got used to the difference in the food and the taste of the water which Jas, my sister-in-law, boiled for us and then chilled, before we drank it. The tea that they made, about six or seven times a day, was brewed using milk from the water buffalo. It was much thicker than cow's milk and had a really sweet taste that multiplied with the amount of sugar that they added to it.

8 **hush-hush** top secret

After the first two weeks of getting used to the differences in our ways of life, I was beginning to settle into things in the village and it wasn't really all that bad.

Inderjit didn't look like he was sixteen years old. He was really skinny and had a bowl haircut that I wanted to laugh at. His trousers were about two sizes too big for him and he usually wore really bright shirts with horrible patterns on them, hand-me-downs from his brothers. His main jobs around the house seemed to be all the general dogsbody type of things. Milking the two cows that my family owned, which were kept out by the house we owned in the fields, feeding and cleaning the water buffalo and walking them out to the waterhole that we had passed by on the first day. He didn't seem to mind any of the work though and was always happy and smiling. I went out into the fields with him during my third week in the village and we had quite a laugh. He kept on asking me questions about England and what it was like to live there. What were white people like and did we all live in mansions and stuff? I tried to explain things like shopping centres and football to him, only I don't think he really knew what I was on about because my Punjabi was so bad. He'd just smile at me, jokingly, and call me *gorah*, white boy. His life had been so different from mine. I mean, Inderjit hadn't even seen an aeroplane yet and he shook his head at me in disbelief when I tried to explain how big a jumbo jet was. I think he thought that I was taking the mickey and went a little funny. 'You *goreh* think we're all stupid,' he told me as he sat on a steep bankside, looking out over one of our paddy fields.

Rice was one of the things that my family grew, alongside corn. It was mainly for selling although they kept some back for food. Punjabis, unlike the Indians further south, didn't really eat rice on a daily basis. The main staple food in the Punjab has always been roti. My uncles also had a few fields in which they grew vegetables for the family. Inderjit took me to see the house out in the fields where a couple of migrant workers kept an eye on things for the family. He explained that the two men were from the south, an area he called U.P. which Ranjit, my brother, told me was Uttar Pradesh, a separate state to the Punjab.

---

7 **hand-me-downs** clothes which an older brother or sister gives to a younger one to wear because they no longer fit – 9 **dogsbody** *(BE)* a person who has to do all the boring or unpleasant things and jobs that other people don't like to do *(Handlanger)* – 18 **mansion** a big, spacious, fancy house, villa – 25 **to take the mickey** to mock or make fun of someone – 32 **staple food** basic food

The house itself, built next to a well, was quite shabby and run-down. The lower floor was all boarded up and some stone stairs ran up one side of it to a living area on the first floor. There were only two rooms up there and a little cubicle that was the washroom, only it had no door or ceiling. Both the rooms and the cubicle came out into an open area which also had an outdoor cooking area with a barbecue-style fireplace. There was no toilet at all. Even back at the house in the main village, the toilet was little more than a bowl that had been placed over a hole in the ground. During my first week in the village I'd had a really bad stomach and the only way to flush the loo was to pour a bucket of water down it, which I found really disgusting. My cousins didn't even bother to use it; they went out into the fields to go to the loo, and then washed themselves using the little streams that ran through the fields for irrigation. It was a bit of a shock for me initially and Harry spent all his time laughing and taking the piss out of me when I headed for the loo.

The well itself was really deep – so deep that I couldn't actually see the water in it. I asked Inderjit if it was dry one day and he laughed at me. He picked up a rock about the size of a tennis ball and threw it down the well shaft. I listened out for a splashing sound which seemed to take ages. When the rock did find the water, the sound was so distant that I wondered what the whole point of the well actually was.

'It must take ages for you to draw the water out,' I said to Inderjit, then felt really stupid when he replied.

'You idiot. We don't use that well any more. Everyone has tube wells now, with motors that pump the water out. We do know *something*, Manjit.'

I tried to laugh off my mistake, to make it seem as though I was only joking and that all along I actually knew how they really got their water, only it didn't work. Inderjit was nowhere near as green as I thought he was. And as if to prove it to me, he pulled out a packet of what looked like little spliffs, rolled in brown paper and tied with string.

'Do you smoke?' he asked me, winking.

'Drugs?' I asked, my eyeballs nearly jumping out of my head.

Inderjit shook his head and started laughing again. 'No, no. Not drugs, although we can get those here too. *Biri*.'

'What's a *biri*?' I asked as he took one out of the thin paper packaging. It looked just like a mini-spliff, about the length of my little finger. Inderjit put it to his lips and pretended to smoke it. In his best English he tried to tell me that it was a cigarette, only the Indian version.

I replied back to him in Punjabi because his English made my grasp of the mother tongue seem A-level standard. 'You smoke these?' I said, pointing at the *biri*.

He looked around to make sure none of my family were about before nodding at me. 'Don't tell anyone.'

Now it was my turn to laugh at him. I'd hardly smoked a fag since the one in the airport, wanting to make sure that my supply lasted as long as possible. To tell you the truth I didn't even want to smoke because of the heat. I spent most of the day dehydrated and drinking loads of Campa Cola and a home-made lemonade that my dad called *skanjvi*. I hadn't managed to pluck up the courage to find a shop in the village that sold cigarettes either, even though my dad had given me a load of bank notes, about a thousand rupees' worth, which worked out to about fifteen quid, max. I just assumed that the shopkeeper would know the family and grass me up. I *had* brought one of my B&H with me though, hoping to find a quiet spot in the fields where I wouldn't get seen. I fished it out of the breast pocket of my short-sleeved shirt and handed it to Inderjit.

'This is what I smoke. English cigarettes.'

'You try one of mine and I'll smoke this,' he said to me, smiling. I looked at the *biri* in his hands and thought, what the hell.

'All right, but if I don't like it, I'm having that one back.'

'OK,' Inderjit said, smiling, as he pulled out a box of matches from the same pocket in which he was hiding his cigarettes. I panicked, wondering who might see us, and he saw me do it. 'It's OK, *bhai-ji* (brother), no-one ever comes out here except me or Jasbir.'

I wondered whether Jasbir, Uncle Gurvinder's youngest son, smoked too. 'Does Jasbir...?' I began, before Inderjit cut me off by nodding and then handing me the sweet-smelling cigarette that he had just lit. It tasted really harsh and I started coughing as soon as I'd had a drag on it. I coughed for about a minute before giving it back to Inderjit and taking back my own cigarette.

'It's good, isn't it?' he laughed. I didn't know about that but it was quite a relief to find that I might have a couple of accomplices for my holiday adventure.

A few days after Inderjit first introduced me to the strange smell and strong taste of a *biri*, I found myself out of normal fags. I

4 **grasp** *here* understanding, competence – 12 **dehydrated** with no water, thirsty – 14 **to pluck up the courage** to force oneself to feel brave *(allen Mut zusammennehmen)*

was sitting on a manjah that I had pulled out on to the veranda and was watching my cousin Avtar's daughters messing about in the courtyard. The older one, Sukhjit, was only three but really clever with it. She had a stick in her hands and was using it to guide her two-year-old sister, Manpreet, as I'd seen Inderjit guide the water buffalo. She'd tap her gently on the bum with it and say '*Chall!*', which is Punjabi for 'go'. Manpreet, far from being upset, was enjoying herself and burst into a fresh set of the giggles every time that her sister commanded her to move. My brother's kid, Gurpal, was just a little older than Sukhjit, and he had trouble walking for longer than ten minutes because he was so big. In fact all the kids that I had seen around the village were really skinny and tough. They played in bare feet and had all these nasty-looking scrapes which never seemed to bother them. Gurpal would cry if you blinked at him the wrong way, sometimes. Ranjit had been joking the night before about leaving him in India to toughen him up and then winked at me. I just laughed at him, knowing that I wasn't about to be left in India by anyone. No way.

    I picked up a bottle of cola that had gone warm in the mid-morning sun and took a swig. It felt strange to be drinking it so early in the day but by about ten the heat started to become unbearable, and that was every day. As I watched the kids play, I noticed that my old man wasn't around. Ranjit and Harry had taken their wives and our mum shopping in Jullundur earlier that morning, and I wondered if my old man might have gone to join them. Every morning so far I had seen him sitting around talking to Uncle Gurvinder about building a new house for the family. Apparently my dad, along with his brothers, had been saving up the money to build something like the house that I liked so much across on the other side of the village – only bigger. The feeling that I got from listening to them was that they were only doing it because the other families in the village, the ones that were rich, were doing it. And, in comparison to, say Naseebo's family, we were rich. I didn't really care though. The house as it was seemed OK but it needed a proper toilet and more than one shower room. And a TV that worked would be nice too. The one in the living room on the first floor was so old that the blokes from the *Antiques Roadshow* would have probably fought over it if it had worked. I liked the idea of having a holiday here because, so far, it had been kind of cool, but living here permanently? Nah, I was already missing

39 **Antiques Roadshow** popular English TV show

McDonald's, going into town, even Evington Road – the shops. I'm a city boy through and through – I need the urban jungle, as all those bad boy rappers like to call it. Living in a village just wasn't my thing at all.

As I sat there lost in my own thoughts, Inderjit appeared with Jasbir in tow and tapped me on my shoulder.

'Shall we go and have a *biri*, *bhai-ji*?' asked Jasbir.

I shrugged my shoulders at him. 'I want to get some proper ones, like I brought with me from England. Can you show me where the shops are?'

Both of them smiled and nodded in unison before gesturing for me to follow them. I tossed the empty bottle into a cardboard box next to the manjah before following them through the courtyard, past Avtar's daughters and out into the village. The main part of the village lay to the north of our house and as we walked I noticed that the further we ventured into the village, the smaller the houses became. Inderjit told me that the houses around the shops were the ones owned or, in most cases, rented by the poorer people, the servants and a few migrant families. Most of them only had a couple of rooms and small courtyards crowded with animals and children wearing ragged clothes. Each house was ringed by a stone wall that looked as though it had been put together by a blind man, the stones jutting out at all angles, unevenly.

'Some of the richer families own them,' said Jasbir. 'They used to be pens for water buffalo and goats years ago.'

The streets were much narrower too and the one that we took weaved its way up into the main square. Every so often we passed alleyways that were so dark and narrow only one of us at a time would have been able to pass through.

'What's down there?' I asked as we passed by. Inderjit looked at Jasbir before answering.

'Let's get your cigarettes and then we'll show you,' he said, winking as he did every time he told me something that he thought was important.

The bloke at the shop where I bought the cigarettes knew Inderjit and Jasbir well. They told me that they always bought their packets of *biri* from him and that he was cool about not telling anyone. I asked them why that was and Inderjit laughed

---

2 **urban** ['ɜːbən] of the town *(städtisch)* – 11 **in unison** simultaneously, together – 16 **to venture** ['ventʃə] to undertake sth dangerous or risky – 23 **to jut out** to stand or lean out from the main body – 24 **uneven** different – 26 **pen** small piece of land used to shut in farm animals – 29 **alleyway** ['æliweɪ] small back-street

and made a suggestive comment about the shopkeeper and someone else's wife. The thought of two people in this village having an affair kind of shocked me because I had always thought that it was something Punjabi people just didn't do. The way you'd hear my old man tell it, the problems of the world were those that were created by white people and Punjabis just didn't get involved. I mean, my family couldn't even mention a pregnant woman without getting all embarrassed about it, and here I was buying fags from a man who wasn't going to grass me up because he was having sex with his neighbour's wife. Here. In my old man's village. I just wished that I had the guts to tell the old man about it, challenge him with it. Hey Dad, you're always banging on about Punjabis having better standards and morals and stuff, well how do you explain this? Forget it. Man, he'd probably have died of a stroke or something.

On the way back out to the fields we passed some more narrow alleyways and gullies. I asked Inderjit again to show me what was down there but he just shook his head.

'I have to do a lot of work today so I can't take you. And you can't go on your own, not down there.'

'Why not, what's so bad about going down those alleyways?' I asked him, before unwrapping my pack of fags, which were called 'Four Square' and looked just like the ones you get in England.

'Bad people, *bhai-ji*. Druggies and whores. It's not good.' He winked at me again, cocking his head to the left.

'Once Onkar went down there and he took some *pheme* (opium),' said Jasbir. 'After they found him, our dads, they broke his legs and locked him up for months.'

'No way,' I began to argue, only to have Inderjit put me right.

'It's really true, that's what happened. Only bad people go down those dark alleyways, looking for loose women or drugs. My dad told me that good Punjabis don't do things like that. Not Jat Punjabis. Only *chamarr* do those things.'

I looked at them both for a moment before shaking my head. I couldn't believe what they were telling me. My old man was such a hypocrite going on about the 'drugs society' and black people all the time. Here, right here in the village he called home, there were drugs and prostitutes and people having affairs, yet I hadn't seen one white person or black person anywhere.

---

1 **suggestive** putting certain ideas or associations into one's mind – 9 **to grass sb up** – 17 **gully** ['gʌli] small narrow valley usually formed by rain water – 26 **to cock** to move a part of your body into a particular direction – 37 **hypocrite** ['hɪpəkrɪt] sb who pretends to have high moral principles that they do not really have

Where was his stupid, racist theory about the social problems in England now?

I began thinking about home again after that and when we got to the fields I told my cousins that I would see them later after they had done their chores. I wanted to be alone so I walked out past all of the rice fields into a grove of mango trees and sat down underneath the one that gave me the most shelter from the sun. I lit up a fag and thought about Ady and Lisa and then, as a huge wave of homesickness took over me, I started to cry as it finally dawned on me, after nearly two months, that Lisa really was no longer my girlfriend, and that I hadn't seen my best friend for so long that I'd almost forgotten the sound of his voice.

Chapter Nineteen
August

Ranjit, Jas and Gurpal spent their final week visiting Jas's family and doing last-minute shopping. They were returning to Leicester two weeks earlier than us because Ranjit had to go back to work. The day that they left Adumpur in a battered old Ambassador taxi was a bad day for me. I envied them and felt homesick like never before. I mean, on and off, I suppose that I had enjoyed it – my holiday – but I wanted to go back home desperately. I wanted to do all the things that I did when I was at home, in Leicester. Catch the bus into town on a Saturday, have a Big Mac, go to the pictures, that sort of thing. I wanted to find out what Ady had been up to since I had been gone, hang out with him, go to some clubs and stuff, just listen to him talking about all his 'runnings'. I wanted to be able to wake up in the morning without being covered in a layer of sweat, to use a normal toilet and a normal shower, eat fish fingers and pizza. Basically, I wanted my old life back, boring as it had been before I came to India.

We'd been here six weeks now – a long time, or at least it felt like it; I'd had enough of all the dust and the heat and the insects that were three times the size of the ones back in England. I did ask the old man about it, about going back with Ranjit, but apparently there was some kind of problem with our return tickets, something about seats being unconfirmed. Our tickets and passports were with some local travel agent in Jullundur

5 **chore** [tʃɔː] work done in the house – 10 **to dawn** [dɔːn] **on sb** to suddenly become clear – 17 **battered** ['bætəd] damaged, broken

being sorted out and the agent had promised my old man that he would get them back to us in a fortnight at the latest. Two more weeks at least. Then again, I had lasted six weeks already, so another two wouldn't make all that much difference. At least that's what I kept on telling myself anyway, to stop my brain from going haywire. Two more weeks of warm cola and dodgy fags. Two more weeks, man.

I spent the time hanging out with Inderjit and Jasbir as they went about their daily chores. Everyone would be up by six at the very latest and we'd all have breakfast together as a family. My dad and his brothers would go off on some business or other and leave the women to prepare the food for the day and to tidy the house and stuff. I'd shower and then go and find Inderjit and Jasbir. We'd leave the house by seven in the morning and go out to the fields to check on the tube wells, or walk the water buffalo down to the lake that I'd seen on my first day in Adumpur. There were the two cows to milk and eggs to collect from the dozen or so hens that were kept out at the farmhouse. By eleven it would be too hot to work in the open and we'd go and chill out under the shade of the mango grove, talking about stuff and smoking fags. Then we'd head back to the village and spend the afternoon wandering around the village or kicking around a football that my old man had got for me from Jullundur. A couple of times I asked Inderjit to take me down one of those forbidden alleys, but he kept on refusing, reminding me about what had happened to Onkar. Eventually I gave up on the idea.

By the time it got to five in the afternoon we'd be back at the house, drinking tea and listening to the stories that our fathers told each other as they got drunk on home-made corn whisky, *dhesi* it's called, or on the really strong-tasting Indian beer which I was allowed to have a bottle or two of. Supper would be at about seven and by eight it would be pitch black and the moths and fireflies would dance in the glare of the light bulbs that lit up the veranda. Each night I pestered my dad about the passports and the tickets and each day he'd laugh and tell me to be patient.

'I'm going to start thinking that you don't like your real home,' he'd reply.

'But it's not my real home.'

At that he'd wink at my uncles and laugh out loud. 'And if the *goreh* kick you out, then where are you going to go?'

---

34 **to pester** to annoy by doing sth again and again

After supper Inderjit and I would go up to the second floor of the house and up again via the stone stairway and out on to the open rooftop. In the darkness it was a bit scary being up there, not knowing how far you were from the edges, around which a half-meter-high wall ran. But at least it gave us some privacy whilst we had a bedtime cigarette and it gave me a well-needed break from my old man's lectures.

It happened during the ninth week of my stay in India. I should have seen it coming a mile off, I really should. Only I didn't. I just kept my eyes closed and ignored all the little signs that were right there in front of my eyes all the time. It was a Tuesday morning and my dad was sitting out at the farmhouse by the well with both of my uncles, reading a hand-written letter. He looked up as I approached the house from the fields with Inderjit in tow, called me over and then continued to read the letter in his hands.

'That agent, Manjit, the one that has our tickets and passports. He had a problem at his office and they have been stolen,' he told me, without looking up. For a moment what he told me failed to sink in, to make any sense, and then suddenly it hit me. I – we were stuck here. Indefinitely. I looked at my Uncle Gurvinder, who nodded and told me that what my father was telling me was all true.

'People here pay lots of money for passports. It is a big business, Manjit,' he told me.

'But...' I tried to say something that would make sense, something that would change the whole situation and make it better, solve the crisis. I couldn't. I had been counting the days that we had left in Adumpur, convincing myself that this week, our ninth week, would be the last in India, that we'd soon be on our way back to Delhi and then on a plane home to England.

'We have to go to Jullundur to sort it all out,' said my dad quietly. 'Maybe even go to Delhi, to the head office for the ticket company. The British Embassy too.'

'When? When are we going?' I started to feel impatient. I wanted to leave right away, get it all sorted out as soon as possible. My life was on hold, like a football player waiting for his dream transfer move to go through. Even though it was so hot and dry, my body felt cold, like someone had swapped my blood for water with ice cracked into it.

21 **indefinitely** [ɪnˈdefənətlɪ] for an unlimited time – 39 **to swap** [swɔp] to exchange

'We are going – Piara, me and your mother. Bilhar and his wife are going to see her family in Phagwara, and you are not needed anyway. We can sort it all out without you being there.'

'But I want to go, Daddy-ji. I'm bored with hanging around in the village. I want to go and see the rest of India.' I glanced at Inderjit, who looked a little bit upset at my words.

'I know, Manjit, I know,' replied my dad. 'All this cannot be helped, can it? It is not my fault that our things have been stolen.'

'I know, Dad,' I began, before he cut me off by raising his hand.

'It is God's will,' he said, shaking his head slowly. I realized that he was about to launch into one of his lectures about kismet and all that other religious stuff and I turned away and started to walk off towards the main part of the house. I had tears in my eyes as I made my way up the stone stairway to the first floor. I didn't even want to go up there but I couldn't face letting any of my family see me cry.

Later on Inderjit tried to cheer me up by buying me a Campa Cola which I was really grateful for. Not because of the heat and the fact that I was thirsty. The bottle felt warmer to the touch than my skin did. It was because Inderjit had no real money of his own which meant that the twelve or fifteen rupees that he had paid for the bottle were far more than he could really afford. When I said as much to him, he laughed and told me that he had scrounged the money from my old man anyway, which made me laugh out loud. We shared one of my fags out in one of the corn fields and then made our way back to the village. The air was cooling by then and a soft breeze made its way across the flat fields which stretched for miles in three directions away from the village. As we entered the courtyard of the house, Harry was wiping his face and neck with a towel. The sweat created damp patches on his cotton top, across his chest and back, and around under his armpits.

'Try washing yourself, Harry. You might even get to like it.' I laughed as I interpreted what I had said in English into Punjabi so that Inderjit would get the joke. Harry pretended that he hadn't heard me. 'Are you deaf or what?' I continued, reverting to English. This time he looked up, giving me the most evil stare that he could manage. I started laughing again and told Inderjit about how smelly Harry got during English summers.

13 **kismet** (*literary*) fate – 26 **to scrounge** [skraʊndʒ] to beg for sth, to persuade sb to give you sth

'You think you're so clever, hey? Try laughing next month when you're still here, innit. See if you get so cheeky then.' Harry had walked over to us and stood face on to me, squaring up like the lead gorilla in the pack. I'd seen that happen once on some nature programme on BBC1 and I always thought of it whenever Harry decided to act like the tough guy.

'Well even if I am still here, I ain't gonna be the only one, am I?' I retorted.

Harry almost began to reply, before catching himself and standing back. I wondered what had made him back off so quickly – it was so unlike him – but then I heard my old man's voice boom across the yard from one of the lower-floor rooms.

'Bilhar!'

'Better go running, Harry – tough guy like you wouldn't want to get whipped by his old man, now would you?' I smirked at him, really piling it on thickly, trying to get him to react, but he didn't. He just whispered that he would sort me out later and then headed for the house. I turned to Inderjit and smiled. 'Did your older brothers ever bully you, too?'

He smiled and then bent forward, rolling up his left trouser leg, to show me a deep scar that ran from his knee all the way up his thigh, about seven or eight inches. It was a kind of dark pink colour against his tanned brown skin and it looked horrible. 'Lally did this to me with a hand scythe about two years ago.'

'Why?' I asked, staring at his scar. It was kind of interesting and sickening at the same time, looking at it.

Inderjit just smiled at me. 'I saw him coming out of one of those alleyways, back near the square, and I threatened to tell my dad.'

'And he did that to you? That's terrible.'

'Well, I told you what happened to Onkar after he went down there.'

'Yeah fair enough, but to do that to you...' I couldn't believe what he was telling me.

'It's all right. It looks a lot worse than it is. The cut wasn't very deep, really. Anyway I got my own back.' He winked at me and smiled again.

'How?' I was curious about how you made up for being stabbed in the leg by your brother.

---

8 **to retort** to answer quickly and sharply – 24 **scythe** [saɪð] farm implement for cutting high grass, grain, etc (*Sense*)

'Lally and Rajvir got married young.' He looked around and put his finger to his lips, before dragging me as far away from the house as possible. I was standing almost eyeball to eyeball with the biggest of the waterbuffalo when he continued his story. 'They didn't want to have children too soon. I heard Lally talking to Rana about it. So Rana gave Lally these things, in a box, and told him to wear them but not to tell my dad.'

I looked at Inderjit in surprise, trying to work out where his little confession was heading.

'So,' he continued, 'I found out where he kept this box of things and I stole one when he wasn't looking. You put them on your...'

I started laughing, nodding my head, as he tried his best to describe a condom to me. 'So you stole one of his condoms?' I winked back at him in the way that he normally winked at me.

'No, no, *bhai-ji*,' he said. 'I took the whole box the next day while Lally was in the fields, and I poked little holes through the foil of every single one, with a very thin needle so that he wouldn't know.' At that he started laughing.

I just looked at him, my mouth wide open, not realizing the full implication of the secret that he had just told me. Then it sank in and I laughed so much that my belly felt it was going to burst and tears streamed down my face without control. Lal's wife, Rajvir, was 'she of the unspoken pregnancy'. What a way to get your own back.

I had taught Inderjit how to greet people in the way that me and Ady did back in Leicester, by balling our fists and touching each other's outstretched hands so that the knuckles collided, the 'cuff' as it was called. After telling me his story and seeing how much it made me laugh, Inderjit offered me his fist, rather than me initiating it as I normally did. I returned his cuff and only stopped laughing when I felt like my insides might explode with the pain.

Chapter Twenty
August

My mum and dad left for Jullundur the next morning with Uncle Piara. Harry and his wife followed suit in the late afternoon sunshine. Baljit had wanted to leave earlier but Harry was having trouble coping with the intense heat during the early

25 **to get your own back** to get your revenge

part of the day, so they had decided to travel later when the breeze picked up and cooled everything down. Thing is, he was so flabby that I wasn't surprised that he felt bad. Harry needed to do some serious exercise.

They were getting into a taxi as I approached and I waved to Baljit. Harry just smiled at me smugly, not bothering to say goodbye, although to tell the truth I wasn't all that concerned anyway. With him and my parents away for a few days I had free rein to do what I wanted, and that was fine by me. I gave him one last look and then headed for the house where Inderjit had already opened two bottles of beer for us. I think that he was looking forward to spending a few days away from the discipline of his old man too.

'This is the life, *bhai-ji*,' he said smiling as I joined him. 'My dad and your dad away in Jullundur and Uncle Gurvinder busy with a new tube well. We will be able to do what we want.'

We sat up late that night, drinking more bottles of beer than we were allowed and smoking cigarettes in the yard when everyone else had gone to bed. I loved the way Adumpur felt and sounded at night – the insects chattering and buzzing, the way that the fireflies appeared as if out of nowhere to fly straight at you, the small lizards that sat on the walls, deadly still, watching and sleeping at the same time. Moths as big as sparrows flapped around the light bulb and a soft, cooling breeze blew in across the flat fields. We sat and talked about England, Inderjit's fascination with my life as strong as the first day that I had spoken to him. It felt like a lifetime since I had arrived in the village, even though it had only been just under two months, and I found myself talking about the silliest and most boring little things as I remembered Leicester.

I told Inderjit about sitting on the top deck of the number 22 bus on the way into town, and the way that people carved messages to each other on the backs of the seats; the no smoking signs that people blew smoke rings at; about getting on for half fare when you were too old to qualify for it. I talked about the way the city centre was so busy on a Saturday, with everyone getting in each other's way; the bad boys that hung out around McDonald's and by the Clock Tower; the smell of the po'boy sandwich stall that was supposed to be authentically New Orleans and the way that I'd buy one of the sandwiches

---

3 **flabby** fat with the skin hanging loosely – 6 **smug** arrogant – 8 **to have free rein** to have the freedom to do whatever you like – 22 **lizard** ['lɪzəd] type of reptile (*Eidechse*) – 39 **po'boy** term used in New Orleans for a sandwich made with French bread

and pretend that I was a tourist visiting the USA and not just this skinny Asian kid that liked to watch people go by and daydream about living a different life to the one that I was.

I think I lost Inderjit after a while but I had stopped caring by then. The way that I was talking about my life made it feel as though it was something way back in my past. I felt like some old bloke sitting in a nursing home, talking about the War and the way that England was so much better before the Blacks and the Pakis arrived – just like one I had met during a primary school visit to an old people's home once. By the time I had stopped talking, Inderjit had fallen asleep on his manjah, and I decided to do the same, not bothering about the mosquitoes which had already left enough marks on me for a lifetime.

The next day Uncle Gurvinder informed us that we were going on a trip north to a place called Anandpur, to visit some famous gurudwaras up in the hills. The journey itself was going to take the best part of a day, he told me, so I had to make sure that I packed plenty of spare clothes.

'We will be back in time for when your parents return from Jullundur,' he smiled.

'So what's this place, Anandpur, like?'

'Beteh, Anandpur is a place to be seen. Beautiful. The gurudwaras are carved out of the hillsides and some of them have been made out of marble.'

'So we'll be a few days?'

'No, we should be back in about a day. Bring your camera, Manjit, it is very beautiful.'

As I packed my shoulder bag I realized that I was looking forward to the trip. I mean, I had hardly seen anything of India outside of Jullundur. It would be fun to travel with Inderjit too. Maybe he'd be able to show me what made his country special, the way that I had described England to him.

I searched the house for Ranjit's camera, which Jas had made him leave behind for me to use. I found it sitting on top of my suitcase, in a side room that my uncles used to store things. I noticed that only my suitcase was in there, alongside some boxes and a battered old fridge that was rusting badly. Harry had obviously taken his with him to his father-in-law's, and my parents' suitcase was in the room where they had been sleeping, a room that Aunt Pritam insisted should remain locked to keep out the mice and the lizards because it was her guest room. I suppose she wanted to make a good impression on her guests.

---

15 **Anandpur** Anandpur Sahib, the Sikhs' holy City of Bliss

We left at ten that morning in a mini-van that my uncle had hired. The driver looked like he was younger than Inderjit and all the way to Anandpur he drove barefoot, never looking in his rear-view mirror nor signalling any of his manoeuvres or turns. Just like the bus that we caught from Delhi, most of the glass from the windows of the van was missing too, all except for the windscreen and the glass in the back door. The seats were better though, but only in as much as they had flat leather cushions on them. Every so often I would see a cockroach or a beetle crawl out of the holes in the leather where it had cracked and broken with age. The van smelt musty too, just like a damp old mattress that my parents had in the garage back at home; it was so mildewy and mouldy that Harry and I occasionally used it as a punch bag – when we weren't using each other's faces that is.

Inderjit and Jasbir had come along too, as well as Uncle Gurvinder and his wife, Harpal, Inderjit's oldest brother, Rana, his wife Sukbir and their two kids, Ranjit and Harjit. The van was pretty noisy, especially as Harjit and Ranjit spent most of the time trying to hang out of the windows, screaming every time Sukbir or Rana pulled them back and sat them down. I sat right at the back, with my arm hanging out of the window. Every time we passed anything going in the opposite direction, I instinctively pulled it back in, remembering just how close the vehicles passed each other.

As the journey went on and we passed through village after village, the land started to become less flat. At one point we drove downward into a deep valley that looked like a dry riverbed or lake. I asked Inderjit about what had happened to the water and he pointed into the distance.

'There is a dam, *bhai-ji*, about five miles from here, that holds back the water and diverts it another way.' I nodded at him and looked out into the valley. It felt strange to be driving through an area that had once been under millions of tons of water, now only held back by a gigantic brick wall. I mean, what if it decided to leak? I kept on thinking the same thoughts until the van driver, who hadn't stopped for a break all day, began the ascent up into the hills along narrow winding dirt roads that in places were only just wide enough for us to pass. As we drove up, higher and higher, and the riverbed started to seem further and further away, the size of the vertical drops grew. At one

---

4 **rear-view mirror** mirror in the car in which you can see what happens behind you – 9 **cockroach** ['kɒkrəʊtʃ] a large insect that feeds on stale food, etc *(Kakerlake)* – 31 **to divert** [daɪ'vɜːt] *(here)* to make sth go into another direction – 37 **ascent** [ə'sent] upward climb

point we rounded a bend and I looked out into nothing but thin air, the land thousands of feet below us, and the other vehicles crossing the valley only tiny dots in the distance. At times I had to look down at my feet as my stomach lurched with nerves, and I became convinced that we would fall off the steep hillside and crash to our deaths. By the time we reached a guest house at the foot of the hills which led up into Anandpur, I was a nervous wreck and I hit my manjah sleeping, not waking until the next morning.

Anandpur was as beautiful as my uncle had promised it would be. We spent the best part of a day wandering up in the hills, exploring the different gurudwaras that seemed to appear right out of the hillsides around each turn. The view as we climbed higher and higher was breathtaking and I spent more time looking out across the valley below us than I did concentrating on the history lesson that my uncle gave us as we reached each site. The temples were amazing too. One of them, the very last one that we got to, was only approachable by climbing up around seventy or so stone steps. It was like two days of football training rolled into one climbing those, and by the time I had reached the top of the moss-covered steps I was dripping in sweat and breathless. The effort was definitely worth it. As I stepped out onto a rock plateau, in front of me loomed a huge white marble temple, the stone reflecting the afternoon sunshine. It was astonishing to think that someone, hundreds of years ago, had scaled these hills and carved a space out of the rocks, before building a monument that was every bit as wonderful as the Taj Mahal. From where I stood, a pathway laid with marble slabs ran about two hundred metres in front of me through a stone archway and into the actual temple itself. As Inderjit and Uncle Gurvinder came up the steps behind me I set off down the pathway, camera at the ready. I took a picture of the pathway itself, a picture of the stone arch, one of the front of the temple – more pictures than I had taken on the rest of the trip. It was so beautiful.

We walked back down at about seven that evening, taking a permanent road that had been built on the other side of the hills. It followed the descent of a fast-flowing river which was ice-blue and gave off a welcome spray of cool water. When I told Inderjit that I'd like to jump into it to cool off, he explained that the water was freezing cold and that it was basically melted

4 **to lurch** [lɜːtʃ] to move heavily and awkwardly – 28 **Taj Mahal** [tɑːʒˈməhɑːl] very beautiful building in Agra, Northern India – 29 **slab** tile

ice which flowed down from the Himalayas and through the Kashmir and Simla valleys into the Punjab. It was an amazing deep-blue colour and I was almost tripping on it as we walked down the hillside towards the village at the bottom where the driver had agreed to meet us. It only took us a couple of hours to get down to him using the actual road, which made me laugh because it had taken us all day to climb up the other side of the hills along the worn old tracks and up the giant stone steps.

'Why didn't we just come up this way?' I asked Inderjit, as we walked past a couple of snake-charmers sitting by the side of the road.

'Where is the fun in that, *bhai-ji*? Think of all the things we would not have seen.'

He had a point because we had seen some really wicked caves and things on the way up, but my aching legs didn't quite see it that way. By the time we reached the village again, I needed my bed and a nice cold drink. I was knackered. Thinking that we would be staying at a guest house for another night, I began to get my backpack out of the van.

Uncle Gurvinder saw me getting my things and laughed. 'No, no, Manjit, we are not staying. We will drive back tonight, after we have had some food.'

'In the dark? Across those hills?' I wasn't *really* hearing this, was I? I mean, it had been bad enough travelling in the van on the way here, in daylight. The thought of having to make the return journey in the dark with a driver who thought he was the Punjabi answer to Damon Hill kind of made me a little nervous.

I imagined dying – all my writing ambitions unfulfilled, not having had a number one record, never having scored a winning Premiership goal for Liverpool. I could see it now, the headlines back in England: potential genius killed in crash. Or teenage sensation's potential tragically taken. My daydream must have turned into a really deep, sleep-dream because when I woke up, covered in sweat with a mouth like an Alsatian's armpit, I was back in the Punjab that I was used to with its flat fields and shanty-style villages and all the potholes in the road – the van rattling and shaking as it avoided people and animals that wandered into its path.

---

10 **snake-charmer** person that uses snakes for entertainment, often using music to train the snake to do tricks – 17 **knackered** [ˈnækəd] totally exhausted, very tired – 27 **Damon Hill** an ex-Formula 1 racing car driver – 35 **Alsatian** German shepherd (a dog breed) – 35 **armpit** hollow place under your arm (*Achselhöhle*) – 37 **shanty** small, roughly built hut

Chapter Twenty-one
August

'No!' I glared up at Uncle Gurvinder and Inderjit, blinking as the tears streamed down my face.

My uncle held onto my arms, stopping me from struggling away from his grip, trying to calm me down, only it wasn't working. I kicked out with one of my legs and found Inderjit's shin, or was it my uncle's? I really didn't care. They were all liars, all of them. In it together from the very beginning and they had tricked me. Like in that game, *Duke Nuke'em*, where you think that you've killed all the aliens on that level, only to have your final life nicked by another alien, hiding behind you. Game over. GAME OVER!

'You're all liars, all of you!'

'No, Manjit, no.' My uncle let go of my arms and stroked my hair, still trying to soothe my anger. 'We didn't know. They didn't tell us anything. Not a thing.'

'Liar! You knew, you all knew. That's why you arranged the trip to Anandpur. To get me out of the way.'

'No, *bhai-ji*, no.' Inderjit had decided to join in. 'We never knew a thing about it, honest. They decided with my father before we went. *Before* we went.'

'So how do you know so much about it all now? You have a dream or something?'

'No, *bhai-ji*. Nothing like that. All I know is what my mum told me about it when we got back.'

'Listen to him, Manjit. It's the truth, son.'

I thought about it for a minute and then decided that I just didn't give a toss who had known. My old man, my mum, Harry, Baljit, they had all tricked me. Made me believe that they had gone to Delhi or to visit relatives in another town. The truth was that they had gone back to England and left me in India.

My uncle held me by the shoulders and shook his head in sympathy. I turned to Inderjit who gave me a concerned look and then I decided that I wanted to be on my own. I shot off towards the courtyard and ended up by the water buffalo, not knowing where I was going or what I wanted to do. The tears started streaming down my face again and my throat felt so dry that I began to dry heave. I bent over and rested my hands just above my knees, waiting for some kind of fluid to pass, only

14 **to soothe** [suːð] to calm – 27 **to not give a toss** *(BE, inf)* to not care at all – 37 **to heave** *(here)* to vomit

nothing came. I just carried on dry heaving and every time that I retched, my head started spinning a little more, until eventually I closed my eyes and the whole of my world started spinning around and around, my head and my chest thumping. My stomach felt as though it had been turned inside out. I stood there like that, swaying, for about ten minutes before the dry heaves stopped and then I felt myself collapse.

Someone, probably my uncle, lifted me and carried me back into one of the bedrooms. I didn't bother to open my eyes at all. Only one thought entered my brain and then swam around and around inside my head. My parents and my brothers had tricked me, duped me into believing that everything was cool. Made me feel easy and relaxed so that I wouldn't see what was right under my nose. I had stopped thinking of them as the enemy, let my guard down, and missed all the clues that in Leicester, I would have seen clearly. All that crap about losing the tickets and passports. Their need to go to Delhi and confirm the seats. Dodgy travel agents. Lies. All to prevent me working out that they had intended on leaving me in India right from the start.

And then I recalled the argument that I'd had with Harry, the day that my old man had told me about our passports being stolen.

'*You think you so clever, hey? Try laughing next month when you're still here, innit.*'

I hadn't even picked up on it then. Now his words stayed in my mind, laughing at me and telling me how stupid I was to have believed them. Not to have seen all the clues. They were like one of those rolling, pounding drum and bass tunes, playing havoc with my brainwaves, over and over and over. No matter how I thought about it all, lying there in the midday heat with my eyes closed, it all came out the same way. They had tricked me. And all along I never saw it coming because like an idiot, I had *trusted* them.

My legs and back still ached from the overnight journey back from Anandpur and my stomach felt like it had been washed out with Domestos. I needed to sleep really badly and the sweat was streaming into my eyes and down the sides of my face. I remember wanting to cry again and then I fell asleep in my clothes, the heat in the darkened room sapping my energy. I dreamt that I had scored a hat-trick at Wembley for Liverpool,

6 **to sway** [sweɪ] to move slowly from one side to another – 12 **to dupe** [dʒuːp] to trick, to deceive sb – 15 **to let one's guard down** to stop being careful and attentive – 20 **to recall** to remember – 28 **to play havoc** ['hævək] **with sth** to destroy or ravage sth – 36 **Domestos** cleaning liquid (brand name)

only to end up on the losing side at the final whistle. I was on my knees, exhausted and crying, trying to work out how much more could go wrong for me.

I spent the next few days in the same kind of state, not really talking to anyone and eating my food alone. Apart from eating all I managed to do was shower or sleep. During the day I sat around in the shade and wrote things to myself in one of the little notebooks that I had brought with me from England. Occasionally I went off by myself, walking out to the farmhouse and smoking cigarettes in the mango grove. I was past caring what my family thought. I mean, what did it matter now? It's not like my mum and dad or my stupid brothers were around to give me any grief. My uncles just left me to my own thoughts and Inderjit and Jasbir tried a couple of times to cheer me up by bringing me drinks or cigarettes, but mostly I just ignored them and kept my thoughts to myself. Uncle Piara had returned the morning after we had arrived back in the village and had tried to get me to listen to his explanation about what my family had done. He had wasted his time too, because all I did was blank him. As far as I was concerned he was as much to blame for it all as my own father and it was too late for him to pretend that he was concerned about me *after* he had helped them to trick me.

I had discovered a disused yard around at the back of the farmhouse, something that Inderjit called the *haveli*. It was walled in and used as open storage for wood and other stuff. At one end there were two small rooms without doors and next to them a chicken coop. Someone had planted two trees in the middle of the dirt yard, about two metres apart. Strung between them was a hammock, like something out of Robinson Crusoe. It twisted and turned when I tried to lie down on it but it became my little private area, that yard, and within a few days I had learnt how to adjust my body weight so that I could sit or lie on the hammock without falling onto the dirt floor. I spent most of my day in there with my little notebook and my fags. The only visitors were Inderjit or Mohan, Naseebo's husband – head of the lower-caste family that worked for my uncles.

Mohan had seemed quite pleased to find me there, like he was glad of the company, telling me that it was nice to see another human face out there. Once he'd worked out that the little pile of cigarette butts that I had hidden in a corner were mine, he kept me supplied with cigarettes, using the money that had been left for me by my father. He was cool, Mohan, and he made me

19 **to blank sb** to ignore sb – 27 **chicken coop** place where chicken are kept – 29 **hammock** ['hæmək] net or cloth hung between two trees to sleep in

smile by telling me stories from his childhood and the things that my old man had done when he was younger. It was nice to get a different viewpoint of life in the village for a change, from a man whose family had never had any money and had always relied on other people to provide work. I asked him about the caste system all the time, and each time that I asked a question, he'd smile his crooked, yellow-toothed smile and tell me that some people were born to be kings and some peasants. That made no sense to me at all and I remember telling him that I believed that everyone was the same and should have the same rights.

'You are right, Manjit. We are all monkeys in the end. It's just that we do not have tails,' he replied, laughing again.

'You see, I knew you'd agree.'

'Ah, but even in the monkey world there are big monkeys and little monkeys. Leaders and followers.'

'So you're a follower-monkey then?' I smiled.

Mohan scratched the greying stubble on his chin before replying, 'Maybe so, Manjit. It is too late for me. This is all I really know. My sons may be different, who knows?'

'Isn't that what you want though, Mohan-ji?'

'What we *chamarr* want and what we are allowed to have, well, that is two different things.'

'Well, I don't think us Jat are any better than you. We just have all the money and the land, and that doesn't make us any better.'

Mohan began to laugh again. 'For such a young monkey you are very wise,' he said.

'Just haven't got a tail.'

'Yes,' he said, lighting a Four Square that I had given to him. 'You just haven't got a tail. That's all.'

For such a skinny little man, Mohan was also very strong and on a number of occasions I was astounded to see just how much weight he could carry. He'd pick up a cast-iron plough like it was nothing and regularly carried several bundles of wood across his shoulders whilst I only just managed to lift one bundle to waist height. I suppose he must have been around forty or something but the muscles in his back and arms looked better than those on a twenty-year-old weightlifter.

'Come, Manjit,' he'd say as I watched him lift things as if they had no weight. 'Let's build up your strength for you. You foreigners are too soft.' When I complained, he'd just laugh at

7 **crooked** ['krʊkɪd] not straight, deceptive – 8 **peasant** ['pezənt] a poor farmer – 33 **astounded** very surprised

me and go on about how easy life was for all the people who had left India and gone to England or America. Thing was, easy or not, it was my real life and even though my conversations with Mohan cheered me up, it was the life that I wanted to have back.

I got a letter from Jas about two weeks after my parents had returned to England without me. It was around the third week of August and I had been in India now since the beginning of June. Aunt Harpal handed me the envelope – one of those blue airmail things – and I wanted to tear it open straight away. I made myself wait until I had reached the privacy of my little hideaway before I finally did though, to make sure that any reaction that I had to it would be in private. The first page of the letter was full of apologies from Jas about what had happened. How she hadn't known anything about what they were planning and how my dad had planned it all from the start. If she had known, she wrote, she never would have encouraged me to travel with them.

Harry had been in on it too, although Ranjit only found out about it on their return to Leicester, which I found hard to believe. Basically they had left me in India so that they could arrange a date for my wedding and get everything planned. My old man had been worried that I might do a runner[23] if I returned to England and had told Jas that it was all for my own good, that the experience would make a man of me. Anyway, the wedding was arranged now, a few months later than originally planned, now set for November, the day of my seventeenth birthday. I was to marry the girl that my father had told me about ages ago – the one who had apparently come over last summer for a visit. He was going to send me a ticket towards the end of September and Ranjit and Harry were going to meet me at the airport. I sat back and thought for a minute. Something was bothering me. Something that I felt I should have picked up on. I thought a little more and then continued to read Jas's neat handwriting.

... you received a letter last week which I collected and opened for you, I hope you don't mind. It was from one of your old classmates, Ady. He wanted to know where you were and what was going on. Apparently he has tried to get in touch all summer. Anyway he gave his new address and asked you to write to him. He also wrote that a girl called Lisa had been asking about you via the Internet. Is that another of your old classmates? Her e-mail address was in his letter too and I have written them both

down for you at the end of this page. Your dad doesn't know that I have written to you and I would appreciate it if you didn't tell him. I just feel so guilty that you have been left there all by yourself when we are all at home. You may not believe me but I really miss having my little brother-in-law around to talk to. I really do. I'm so sorry about what has happened. I honestly didn't know that they were planning any of this.
See you in a few weeks
Love Jas.

Once I had reread it all, I folded the letter and put it in the breast pocket of my short-sleeved shirt, removing my fags at the same time. I lit one with a flimsy match that had more sulphur on its head than wood on the stick and settled back into the hammock. A whole football team of little thoughts started playing a match in my head and I tried to make sense of them all. Ady, Lisa. Had Ady e-mailed her? Or Sarah? Were they in regular contact? Where was she – still in Australia? Was Ady a dad yet? Had he realized that I was missing? Had he told anyone else?

And then a problem hit me. My passport. For me to get back home I needed to have my passport. That meant that they couldn't have taken it back with them, and it certainly couldn't have been stolen by some dodgy travel agent. It had to be in the house somewhere, hidden from me by Uncle Piara. I made a mental note to try and find out where before I re-lit my cigarette and thought about Lisa for the first time in weeks.

I must have fallen asleep on the hammock again because I was woken by the sound of a booming voice. Something about the way that it sounded was familiar although I couldn't quite identify what. As I blinked into the sunlight I tried to work out who was standing beside my hammock. The man repeated himself and I worked out what he was saying to me.

'Who's this monkey sleeping in my hammock?'

His voice was really deep, or at least it seemed that way to me and something about the whole situation was strange. His voice sounded familiar but not, and I felt immediately confused. Sitting up and looking at him, I saw that he was about my father's height and had long, curly hair down to his shoulders – like mine would have been if I let it grow. He was wearing a pair of blue jeans that looked like 501s, a blue Adidas sweatshirt and a pair of Nike trainers that I'd never seen before – and I knew my trainers. I blinked at him in the sunshine and tried to work

12 **flimsy** thin, without substance

out who he was and why he was so normally dressed, or at least normal in the way that I understood it.

'Come along, out of my bed, young man,' he said, smiling at me.

Again, he sounded familiar. My brain was playing a second period of extra time trying to work out who he was when I saw Mohan approaching. I raised my eyebrows at him and then looked at the man in front of me. Mohan came over, grinning like an idiot and gestured to the man.

'Say hello to your youngest uncle, Manjit.'

I looked up at him and blinked some more.

'And get yourself out of my bed.' He was grinning too, my uncle, and as I muttered a weak greeting to him I realized what was so strange about the whole situation. Mohan and I, we were talking in Punjabi. My uncle had said everything in perfect English. As I realized this he smiled at me and he winked, reading my thoughts before they connected to my mouth.

'Yes, I am your youngest uncle and, yes, I can speak English. It's nice to meet you, Manjit.' He smiled and offered me his hand. 'I'm Jag.'

Chapter Twenty-two
August

The day after I first met Uncle Jag he left to visit some friends, so I didn't get a chance to talk to him at first. He intrigued me, partly because he was the black sheep of the family – the one who was hardly ever mentioned – and partly because he looked to me like a normal bloke, like the people back at home. He also spoke English without an Indian accent.

He was gone for two days, time which I spent asking questions about him of anyone who would answer. Inderjit and Jasbir didn't really know much; most of what they told me was just the two of them parroting the stuff that they had been told by their parents. Inderjit told me that Uncle Jag was a strange man, not proud of the family like everyone else, not willing to lend a hand with the crops or the upkeep of the house and spending most of his time in other countries. His father, my Uncle Piara, had warned Inderjit away from Jag, calling him a bad example for the rest of the family.

22 **to intrigue** [ınˈtriːg] to fascinate – 30 **to parrot** to repeat after sb without thinking (like a parrot) – 32 **to lend a hand** to help

'He is not a good man,' Inderjit told me as we sat in the mango grove smoking cigarettes. 'There is too much rubbish going on in his head. My daddy-ji told me that he has all these fancy ideas about things and is not proud to be a Jat like we are.'

'He has strange ideas about our traditions and our religion,' added Jasbir, flicking a matchstick into the air. The midmorning sun was sweltering again and I had a line of sweat heading its way across my forehead just below my hairline. Even in the shade, the heat was clinging to me like a jacket. I sat and smoked my fag and thought some more about my youngest uncle.

Then I remembered listening to a conversation that my old man had once had, over the phone with Uncle Piara and what had followed. I had been about eleven at the time. The old man had sworn down the long-distance line at his brother. 'We don't need Jag's dirty money,' he had shouted before slamming the phone down and storming into the kitchen to look for his bottle of Teacher's whisky. I remembered waiting for him to calm down so that I could ask him about all the fuss but he just kept on swearing to himself as he walked into the living room and sat down in his favourite chair, a full tumbler of whisky in his hands, eyes pointed at the telly. He went on and on about the family name, his father's honour. About how someone should have held someone else down and beaten him into a real man.

All I'd wanted to know was who this 'Jag' actually was and when I eventually managed to get a word in, all I did was start him off again on one of his rants about family honour. He told me that in every family there was always one who wanted *chol* (rice) when everyone else had to eat roti: something that he would accuse me of later in my life. When I asked Ranjit, he told me Uncle Jag was a bad man who didn't like the rest of the family.

Harry's contribution was predictable. 'He's gay anyway, innit. The poof,' for which he got a smack in the mouth from Ranjit. Not because Ranjit wasn't homophobic, oh no. It was because, according to my eldest brother, being gay was something Punjabi men didn't do. Especially not in *our* family.

'So what has he actually done?' I remember asking.

'He's sent some money to Uncle-ji in India, innit, to buy some lands with. After all the time he ain't been in the family, now

---

4 **Jat** peasant caste of northern India and Pakistan – 7 **sweltering** extremely hot – 26 **rant** long, excited talk, complaint – 34 **homophobic** hostile towards homosexuals

he wants everything. Daddy-ji won't let him though cos it ain't right, is it. He just wants to take our lands and that, you know.' I just nodded at Ranjit, pretending that I understood what it was all about, so that they'd think of me as a grown-up and not a kid. That had been my earliest recollection of Uncle Jag's name being mentioned in our house and I suppose that it had shaped the way that I thought about him and the person that he was. To tell you the truth, until he'd told me to get out of his hammock in perfect English, I hadn't really given him that much thought. Now he was fast becoming the only intriguing person in my entire family, someone who had broken away and done what he had wanted and not what the family expected of him. I was dying to find out some more.

Later on that day I was helping Aunt Harpal with some chores around the house and I asked her about my wayward uncle. She gave me a funny look as she swept dust and dirt from the living room out onto the veranda that ran across the ground floor of the house. She waited until she had finished sweeping before answering me.

'Jag is a very strange man. We think that he has a wife and children somewhere but no-one is really sure. He spends a lot of time in Australia and other places, travelling and working, I think. I don't really know and he never talks to me or anyone else in the family about it.'

'But he seems quite nice, Aunti-ji,' I replied, trying to defend him even though I didn't really know him.

'What you see, Manjit, is only one part of him. He can be very nice but also very uncaring. When your grandfather died he didn't even send a letter, never mind come back for the funeral.'

'Maybe he didn't know,' I said, trying to remember when my grandfather had died.

'Beteh, he knew. Your Uncle Piara sent him a telegram to let him know. He was working in Saudi Arabia at the time.'

'Saudi Arabia?'

'Yes, beteh. He has worked in many different countries – just never his own.'

'But what does he do?' I asked, watching Aunt Harpal flicking a fly from her face and then smiling.

'Who knows, beteh. He tells no-one and no-one asks him about it.'

5 **recollection** memory

My face must have shown my surprise and lack of understanding of her attitude towards my youngest uncle. She laughed and then said something about helping her clean out the water-buffalo feeding-pen. I decided to wait until my uncle got back from his trip so that I could ask him for myself.

* * *

On the morning that Uncle Jag was due to return, I went down to the haveli earlier than usual. It must have been around eight in the morning and the sun was trying to break through the white clouds above me as I lay in the hammock. It was already very warm and I was glad that I had decided to wear a light cotton T-shirt and some shorts. It was going to be yet another scorching day, just like every other that I had seen since arriving in India.

According to Inderjit and Mohan it should have rained by now and they were worried that the crops would suffer if the rain stayed away. Personally, I was thankful for the drought because it kept both of them busy in the fields and I wanted some time to myself, alone to think. I had Jas's letter with me and I read and reread the part about Ady before looking at his new address. He was living in Highfields, on Cedar Road, where we used to mess about as kids. Maybe he had moved in with his brother. Or was he working and renting somewhere of his own now?

I really needed to write to my best friend, to explain where I was and what had happened. Just be able to get all of my feelings off my chest in the way that I was used to. Thing was, the shops in the village didn't sell airmail envelopes and the post office had been closed since I got there. The nearest one was in Jullundur and I wasn't allowed to leave the village on my own. Uncle Piara had refused to give me an envelope when I had asked, telling me that I had to wait, on my old man's orders, until I got back to England. I wasn't allowed to write any letters or to phone anyone and I had no idea what they had done with my passport.

As I lay there thinking about it I began feeling very depressed. I tried to cheer myself up by thinking about Leicester and the fun I had as a kid, but it didn't work. The more that I thought about positive things, the more the negatives outweighed them. I ended up lying on the hammock staring up at the sky,

12 **scorching** very hot – 16 **drought** [draʊt] period without rain

convinced that, despite the sunshine that beamed down, a personal grey cloud was following me around.

I must have fallen asleep because when I awoke the sun was right above me, burning down over the fields and the houses, dry and hot and airless. I felt like I was suffocating, my head throbbing. Each time I closed my eyes I saw blood-red dots and sweat was pouring from me. I fell out of the hammock as I tried to get up and the force of my landing on the dry floor cut gashes across both my knees. I blinked into the sun, my eyelids faster than a camera shutter at a show-biz exclusive and then tried to get up, slowly. My head spun around as I brushed the sandy dust away from my cuts. All of a sudden I felt I was going to puke. The cut to my left knee poured blood, trickling slowly down the hair of my shin. I closed my eyes, trying to clear my head, but all I saw was more blood and blinding dots that flashed red then yellow, then red then yellow. I opened my eyes and tried not to sway from side to side as my stomach turned over. The haveli was about two hundred metres behind the main house and I started to make my way back slowly. The walk should have been a short one, only every time that I put weight on either foot, I felt a shooting pain in the shin and knee. I felt like I had been walking for ages by the time that I reached the house. I walked around to the front and into the courtyard, the blood from my left knee now in my trainer and my eyes watering from the pain. My head throbbing in the dry heat, I looked around for a member of my family.

The courtyard was empty except for the water buffalo in the corner. Hobbling across the yard and on to the veranda, I caught raised voices, shouting at each other in Punjabi. One of them belonged to Uncle Piara and the other to Uncle Jag. They were in the living room that I had helped Aunt Harpal to sweep out the day before and I decided to hobble towards them, trying not to collapse as my head swirled around like water going down a plug hole. As I reached the door their words became clear.

'... defending the family name. That's all I'm doing.'

'It's called kidnap in any other country,' shouted Uncle Jag.

'What do you know with your stupid ideas, Jagtar? It is for his own good. It's something that we should have done with you at the same age. You might be a real Jat now.'

'But you never could...'

'And look at what you have become. A disgrace!' replied Uncle Piara. They both took a breath before Uncle Jag answered.

5 **to suffocate** to die because of not being able to breathe properly – 6 **to throb** to beat, pulse – 8 **gash** wide cut – 32 **to hobble** to walk with difficulty, limp

'He's just a child. What is wrong with all of you? Why can't you let people alone to be what they are?'

'What, so they can end up whoring around the world like you?'

'You don't know anything about my life, Piara. Nothing.'

'And I don't want to...'

'I live my life for me. Not you. Not our father. Not the family honour. Me!'

'You were always selfish, even when you were a child. If our father...'

'Yes, he would have made a man of me, wouldn't he? Just like he did with the rest of you. Beat you every day to make you a real Jat.'

'Maybe he didn't beat you enough!' shouted Uncle Piara as I opened the door, quickly realizing that they were arguing about me. Both of them looked up and I tried to smile, only my legs gave way and the thumping in my head made my ears pop. I saw them both run towards me as I fell sideways against the bare stone wall.

'It's called sunstroke, young man.' I lay on a manjah in the darkness of one of the bedrooms with Uncle Jag sitting beside me. He had woken me with a glass of water and was holding the back of his hand flat against my sticky forehead.

'Have I got a temperature?' I asked him, my voice dry and cracked.

'I hope so, Manjit,' he smiled as he pulled his hand away. 'Otherwise you're dead.'

My head was still throbbing, only the ache was much duller than it had been earlier, concentrated in the back of my neck. I tried to get up and the effort made my head spin.

Uncle Jag pushed me back down and smiled again. 'Keep still, Manjit. Now is not the time to start walking around. Sunstroke can be a very serious thing.'

'Uncle-ji?'

'Yes?'

'Can I ask you a favour?' I tried to smile too but couldn't manage more than a little grimace before my neck began to ache.

'Yes you can, Manjit.'

'Will you call me Manny?'

'Manny?'

28 dull (*here*) less sharp

'Yeah. I hate being called Manjit.'

He smiled some more then got up and walked over to a cupboard set into an alcove in the wall. Opening it he took out a packet of paracetamol and then brought two of the pills over to me. 'Sure, I'll call you Manny but you've got to do me a favour too.'

'What?' I asked, taking the pills from him and waiting for him to pass me the glass of water on the floor by my manjah.

'Don't call me Uncle-Ji. In fact don't call me Uncle either. Just Jag will do. I'm not your father.'

'But you are my elder,' I replied, lifting my head so that I could swallow the pills with a drink of water as my uncle held the glass to my mouth.

'All that tradition about elders and youngsters. It's all so stupid. To say "ji" is to show me respect, regardless of whether I've earned it. Or whether I'm worthy of it. People shouldn't automatically deserve respect just because they have lived longer than someone else. People are born to deserve respect. All people. It doesn't matter if they are one or one hundred years old.'

I thought about what he was saying for a while and then shut my eyes to try to rest. The muscles all over my body ached and I remembered the deep cuts that I had on my knees. I reached down to feel them and found that they had been bandaged.

'I did that earlier, after you passed out,' said Uncle Jag, gesturing towards my knees with his hand. I opened my eyes and looked over at him remembering too the fight that he had been having with my eldest uncle.

'What were you two fighting about?' I asked.

'You.'

'I thought so; I can only remember bits of it.'

'Get yourself some more rest and I'll fill you in on the rest later. Maybe tomorrow.'

'OK,' I croaked as my eyes began to feel heavy and the dull ache in the base of my neck started to get stronger. 'Uncle?'

'Jag. Not uncle,' he said, getting up and walking towards the door.

'Jag. Thank you.' I was falling asleep as I said it, the effects of my sunstroke obviously still strong. I think that I heard him say 'you're welcome' as he shut the door behind him.

---

3 **alcove** niche – 32 **to fill sb in on** to inform sb – 34 **to croak** to speak in a deep, rough voice

Chapter Twenty-three
August

'What do you do then?'

We were sitting out on the veranda, Uncle Jag and me, a couple of days after I had passed out with sunstroke. Midmorning, the house was deserted and, as it had rained for the whole of the previous day, the air was now a lot cooler with clouds low in the sky.

Uncle Gurvinder had taken his family to a religious service at his in-laws' village and everyone else was either away or out in the fields doing some chore or other. It was a Saturday, I think. I can't be sure because living in Adumpur had caused me to lose track of the days. It wasn't like being in Leicester where you could turn on the TV and find out just from what was on what day of the week it was. Every day was pretty much the same and my family all did the same routine things each day.

The cool breeze came as such a welcome relief from all the heat of the previous weeks. We were drinking tea that had been brewed using the thick creamy milk of water buffalo cows. Uncle Jag had thrown in some spices and a lot of raw cane sugar, so raw that when you touched it your hands became sticky; the resulting taste and smell was like burning treacle with garam masala.

Uncle Jag was wearing a traditional Punjabi outfit and had let his beard grow out so that he looked surprisingly similar to my old man, back when my old man was thin and had hair and normal, non-yellowing eyes – like the pictures on his earliest passport that I had seen in his trunk.

'What do you mean exactly when you say "do"?' Jag replied, taking a sip of his tea.

'You know, like work and stuff,' I said, setting my cup down on the stone floor. My uncle looked out into the courtyard, like he needed to consider what I was asking really carefully before replying.

'I do lots of things, I suppose,' he replied after a moment.

'OK. So your English, how come it's so good compared to everyone else's?'

'Easy. I got myself an education and then went away rather than stay here and become a Jat.'

---

4 **deserted** empty, without people – 5 **previous** last few, preceding – 17 **to brew** [bruː] to make a drink by heating the ingredients (beer) or by pouring boiling water over them (tea) – 18 **cane sugar** raw sugar, as it grows in the field – 20 **treacle** [triːkl] *(BE)* thick, sweet, black liquid obtained from the sugar plant *(Sirup)*

'So you left here then?'

'Yes. I left to go to Delhi, to university although I did go to school in the village and then to a college in Chandigarh.'

'And what about Uncle Piara and Uncle Gurvinder? Did they go to school?'

Jag thought about this for a moment and smiled. 'Piara and Gurvinder are chips off the old block or whatever the correct term is. Education won't help to run the farm, so what use is it to them?' He smiled again, only I think that this time it was more for his own benefit than for mine.

'Well, I suppose if they wanted to be farmers...'

'But that's just it. Education can help them with the farming. I can help them. I've got a first-class degree in Agricultural Engineering and Systems – and a Doctorate in Chemical Engineering. The Punjab doesn't supply a quarter of India's wheat and nearly a third of its dairy products without the benefits of education.'

I had been in India for weeks and it was only now by talking to Uncle Jag that I had learnt anything about the place. I decided to press him some more, now that he was on a roll.

'You said that you could help them. How come you don't?'

'They don't ask me to and they don't want my help. I've offered it before.'

'Yeah, you sent them some money or something,' I said.

He looked surprised that I knew and raised his eyebrows. 'More than once, Manny. And they just give it back to me. God knows, I've got enough of it. It didn't come easy, though. I was stuck out in the field when your grandad died and it took me three weeks to get the telegram. I didn't even make his funeral.'

I remembered what Aunt Harpal had said about my uncle being uncaring and selfish. The look of hurt on his face as he spoke about his father was anything but. I was going to press him but I decided it was a sensitive subject and left it alone.

'What you mean, you're loaded – I mean, rich?'

'Relatively I am, I suppose. I've just got a lot of disposable income. I work for the Agricultural department of the Australian government. On irrigation systems. Environmental stuff.'

'That sounds important,' I said, realizing that he had answered my next question about where he lived.

---

3 **Chandigarh** Indian city about 240 kilometres north of New Delhi – 7 **to be a chip off the old block** to be like your parents – 16 **dairy products** milk, cheese etc – 35 **disposable income** the money that is left after all deductions and payments every month for you to spend freely (*verfügbares Einkommen*)

'It's on a contract basis. I work for six months or a year on a project and then I do something else.'

'Like what?'

'Like travel and things.' He picked up his bag again and started to rummage in it.

'Such as?'

'Just things, Manny. I'll tell you some other time.' He looked as though he meant it too, like I had pushed him too far, only I still had loads more to ask, thanks to my naturally inquisitive mind, with which I used to drive Mr Cooke, my old teacher at school, mental. Always following a question with a question.

'So you moved to Australia after you got all your degrees and stuff?' I waited for him to reply but all he did was pull a packet of cigarettes from his bag.

'Do you smoke?'

'Er ... No, Uncle-ji – I mean, Jag. No, I ... er ... don't.'

'It's OK, Manny. Mohan told me.'

'Did he?' I replied, feeling a little let down by Mohan who had promised not to tell anyone.

'It's all right, Manny. I'm going to have one anyway and if you can forget all your little hang-ups about what you can and can't do in front of your family, feel free to have one too. I've got four hundred more in my suitcase. I shouldn't really encourage you – I wish I *didn't* smoke, actually, for my health. But you *are* old enough to make your own choices.'

I couldn't believe it. I was still nervous about taking a cigarette but I took one, lit it, and did something that I never thought I'd ever do. Sat with an older member of my family and smoked.

'So you moved to Australia after your degree?' I asked again after a while.

'No. I got a job with the Agriculture Ministry in Delhi and then moved to Mumbai. After that I went to work for a big oil company in Saudi and then Kuwait.'

'Saudi Arabia?'

'Yes, only the company was too interested in ruining and polluting the land, so I left and went to China for a year. After China I went with a British company to New Zealand and then travelled to Fiji. Oh and Japan in-between.'

'Wow, you've been everywhere, man. That's so wicked.' I was impressed.

'Wicked?' This time it was my uncle's turn to look confused.

'Yeah, you know – wicked, as in great. Wonderful.'

9 **inquisitive** [ɪnˈkwɪsətɪv] questioning, curious, interested

'Ah, I see. Bad meaning good. Very American street style,' he laughed.

'Have you been there too?' I asked.

'No, not yet. But I'm going there soon. I'm going to be in London too, later in the year, for a conference on the environment.'

'So where do you live now?'

'Australia. In Sydney and in Canberra, although I have to travel all over with work.'

'That's wicked ... I mean, great,' I replied.

'No, what is wicked is that I've spent the last hour telling you all about what I do, and you've escaped without telling me a single thing about your own life.' He poured both of us some more tea from a steel thermos on the floor. 'Tell me everything. And don't feel like I'm going to disapprove of anything that you say. I've got a very open mind.'

I took a deep breath – and told him everything about Leicester and school and Ady and Lisa. All the stuff about how my dad and Harry hit me all the time, or threatened it. All the emotional blackmail stuff with my mum. And arranged marriages.

And how to cheat out of them.

The rest of the family were back by the early evening and Uncle Jag had gone off with Mohan to attend to some business in the village. I had spent the whole afternoon chatting to Jag about how desperate I was to get out of Adumpur, if only I could find my passport and get a ticket back to England. Uncle Jag had encouraged me to speak about what I thought and felt and it had been just like having a real conversation with Ady back in Leicester. I was in a much better mood now – especially after Uncle Jag had then promised to help me escape back to England.

He had told me to leave it with him, that he would think up a plan of action for me. It had felt so good to talk to someone who didn't think that leaving me in India against my will was anything other than a cruel and illegal thing to do, and I began to believe that my life was my own again. It felt wicked.

We ate at around seven that evening by which time the cooling breeze of the earlier part of the day had given way to a warm and sticky night. We were coming into late summer and the temperature had cooled down quite a lot, although it was still as high as during a good English summer. We were eating *saag*, a vegetable dish made with spinach along with thick yellow roti that was made using corn flour. Aunt Pritam made the food and had thrown fresh green chillies into the *saag* which meant that I needed to drink water with almost every mouthful. Inderjit sat on the floor opposite, his legs crossed and his steel tray of food sitting in his lap. As I ate he kept on smiling and winking at me, fanning his hand in front of his mouth, joking at my expense. Jasbir had finished eating and was busy teasing his older brothers' daughters whilst his parents sat on the floor next to Uncle Piara and Aunt Pritam. Lal and his wife sat behind me, with Onkar and his wife, Balbir – and behind them Rana's wife Sukbir fed her two kids, Ranjit and Harjit whilst chatting to Jaswant, cousin Avtar's wife. It still felt strange to me, after all my time in India, to sit down to eat with so many people. It was like double the number of people I ate with back at home and I had thought that just my immediate family was big enough.

In one sense, I suppose, it was all right having so many people around all the time, especially for the kids. Different people to play with. But at the same time I found it rather claustrophobic – all these people, every day, and all with the same ideas. Traditional people who couldn't see my point of view, or wouldn't. It did my head in. It meant that all I was doing was going through the motions, you know, having the same conversation ten times a day. That was what made Uncle Jag so special. Made him stand out from the rest. And just as I was thinking all of this, he walked into the yard with a big smile on his face and a bag full of sugar cane stalks which he handed out to the kids as a dessert. I waited until he had got himself some food and then, leaving my own dishes where they were, I went over to where he sat on the veranda.

'Did you think about what we were saying before?' I asked, as he dipped a piece of roti into his *saag*.

'Don't worry, Manny, it's all under control,' he said before putting the roti into his mouth with a smile.

'And it'll be cool with them?' I nodded in the direction of Uncle Piara.

Jag chewed on his food a little more, swallowed and then drank some water. He smiled at me and then looked over at his brother. 'Manny, this is about what *you* want, not what they expect of you. I'll help you, I said I would. You let me worry about what they think. OK?'

I nodded.

21 **did my head in** *(inf, fig.)* made me angry and confused – 22 **to go through the motions** to do sth mechanically, without real interest

'Good, now go and get me a bottle of beer please and, after I've finished eating, we'll go up on to the roof and I'll tell you my plan.'

I nodded, grinning like The Joker in *Batman*. What had he planned since our conversation earlier in the day? Whatever it was, one thing was for sure. I was ready to get the hell out of Adumpur and out of India. Back home to Leicester to find my cheat and step on up to the next level.

Chapter Twenty-four
August/September

The plan took just over a week to put into place. Getting hold of my passport without my older uncles finding out should have been the hardest part but Inderjit decided, unwittingly, to make it the easiest, letting its location slip over a bottle of beer. I don't think that he was supposed to tell me, judging by the look on his face when he did. He looked just like a kid caught with his hands in the sweet jar, and I had to tell him five or six times that I wouldn't go blabbing to his old man. I told him that I just wanted to know where it was. It's not like I'm going anywhere, is it? I told him. The combination of my sincerest look and another beer and half a pack of cigs did the trick, convincing him that he wouldn't get into trouble.

I told Uncle Jag, who sneaked it from its hiding place amongst the important papers that Uncle Piara kept in a locked chest in his bedroom – under his bed. I didn't feel bad either. The sodding thing was mine after all. I was in a wicked mood. Now that we had my passport, it was just a case of us getting the hell out of Adumpur, without my family noticing that we were gone.

Later on I dozed off until the sound of Mohan clanking around in the yard made me sit up.

Mohan was covered in dust, his old clothes soaked through with sweat. Behind him, in a pile shaped like a pyramid over a metre high, were a load of steel pipes – part, I guessed, of the irrigation system involved in the tube wells that were all over the land my family owned. I couldn't be sure though, because what I knew about farming you could fit on the back of a twenty-pence piece! I jumped off the hammock, pulled a cigarette from my pocket and offered it to him.

'No thanks.' He eyed the cigarette in my hand and then pulled out a paper package of *biri* from his own pocket. 'I can't let myself become used to your foreign *biri*. How will I afford to buy them when you are gone?'

---

13 **unwittingly** accidentally, not on purpose – 18 **to blab** to talk, to report – 23 **to sneak** [sni:k] to take away secretly, to steal – 25 **sodding** *(BE, inf, vul)* damn

'I'll send you some,' I replied, smiling and catching the matchbox Mohan threw at me after lighting up. 'Has Uncle Jag told you what we are going to do?' I continued, wiping sweat from my forehead with the back of my hand.

'He has told me, Manny-ji. I am the one who has made all the arrangements.' He shook his head from side to side, taking a long drag on his *biri* before walking up and placing his hand on my shoulder. 'I am happy for you, now that you are going home soon. Happy but sad too, Manny-ji. You are a good friend to an old monkey like me.'

'I'm going to miss you, too, Mohan. You've been really kind to me, more than most of my family. And you have to stop calling me "ji". I'm not better than you just because I was born into a different caste.'

'If I do not call you "ji", will you do me a favour when you get back to England?'

'Yes, of course I will.' I wiped yet more sweat away from my forehead and felt a fly come away onto my hand: one thing that I was definitely not going to miss.

'Will you send me some photos, the ones that you have taken with your camera?'

'Yes, Uncle-ji, I promise.'

'Good. Good. I do not have any photographs of my family,' he said.

I remembered going to the open courtyard and two-roomed shack that his family lived in. I had taken photos of his wife, Naseebo, and their kids, and some of his own father, who was bent over with old age and had wispy tufts of white hair growing in patches on his head, his eyes clouded over with cataracts like smudged grey chalk on a blackboard. They had all stood to attention when I took the pictures, really formal poses and serious faces. Uncle Jag told me that they posed like that because they saw having a photograph taken as something important and that they were trying to make a good impression on anyone in England who might see them. Apparently they thought that those stiff, formal poses were what were expected.

'We have never had a camera in our family,' said Mohan, breaking my thoughts. 'We are just poor people.'

He spoke with an air of resignation. It wasn't like he was trying to make me feel sorry for him, so that I would give him something. He said it in a matter of fact way as if he believed that he could never change anything. I had already decided to

26 **shack** hut – 28 **wispy** thin – 28 **tuft** bunch of hair or grass – 29 **cataract** part of the eye that has gone blind – 30 **smudged** [smʌdʒd] having dirty marks

leave him my camera and the couple of rolls of film that I hadn't used up. I mean, it was no skin to me – the camera wasn't even mine. And to tell you the truth, being in India had made me think about all the things that I took for granted. I looked down at my mashed-up trainers and decided that I was lucky to have them at all, never mind the ability to buy a new pair if I wanted to. Most people in India had nothing. They wore the same clothes until they fell off and made do with basic food, basic everything. In Adumpur there were a few rich families, with cars and big houses – stuff bought with money that their fathers and grandfathers had earned in England and America and Dubai and Saudi Arabia. But most of the people were poor. I could get another camera anytime I wanted. The camera meant ten times as much in Mohan's world as it did in mine. That was one of the best lessons I took from my time in India. Making relative comparisons, Uncle Jag had called it.

I looked down at my trainers again and then over to Mohan and the cracked brown leather slip-ons that he always wore, with no socks, the dust caked to his ankles, and the feeling of guilt started up again. Were trainers really so important?

Mohan must have read my mind because he put his hand on my shoulder and laughed. 'Do not worry, Manny. It is the way of the world that some people have money and most people do not. How would the world work otherwise?'

Uncle Jag sat discussing land prices with Uncle Gurvinder on the veranda later that evening. I watched him from the yard where my cousins – Inderjit, Jasbir and his brother Onkar – were working on the engine of the family tractor. Onkar had stripped it down and was in the process of cleaning the parts and oiling them, describing to us exactly which part performed which task and where it went. Inderjit and Jasbir were engrossed in it all but my mind was elsewhere, dreaming about the trip to Delhi and about how it would feel to finally get off the plane back in England. Cousin Avtar's daughters, Sukhit and Manpreet, broke my thoughts. Manpreet had a stick in her hand and was poking a new water buffalo calf with it. The calf was trying to back away but its path was blocked by the size and weight of its mother. As Manpreet teased and prodded the calf, its skinny legs gave way and it toppled forward. Manpreet squealed with delight at her game and her elder sister, Sukhjit, decided to join in. Manpreet then turned the stick on her sister, to the obvious relief of the calf which pulled its chain around and as far underneath its mother's flank as possible. The cow, its head in the water trough, didn't even notice. A sharp slapping sound made the cow look up and then screaming and crying took over. Sukhjit had knocked Manpreet over.

I walked over to Manpreet and held out my arms. She stood crying for about thirty seconds, looking around to see if anyone else would come to her aid, before realizing that I was her only choice. I picked her up and went over to the veranda, handing Manpreet to her mum, Jaswant. She smiled without saying a word and then looked away.

'Did your uncle-ji hit you, Manpreet?' asked Aunt Harpal, who was sitting next to Jaswant. I started to defend myself before realizing that my aunt was teasing me. 'I hear that you are going to make paratha for us one morning?' she continued, looking highly amused.

'Huh? Paratha?' I said. I didn't have a clue what she was on about. Paratha are like double chapatis filled with potatoes or herbs and spices.

'Yes he is,' said Uncle Jag from behind me. I turned around and gave him a questioning look before asking him in English what he was on about. Rather than explain, he just smiled and winked at me before continuing in Punjabi to Aunt Harpal. 'He wanted me to show him how to make them so that he could say thank you for looking after him.'

I glared at my uncle who just carried on smiling.

'And *you* know how to make paratha?' asked Aunt Harpal, mocking my uncle.

'When you spent so much time living by yourself, you have to learn these things,' he replied, smiling.

'If you had married a nice Punjabi girl, Jagtar, then maybe you would have had someone to make these things for you, yes?'

Uncle Jag's smile wavered a little bit but he kept his cool. He turned to me and gestured with a hand. 'Maybe Manjit here can make paratha for *his* wife.'

I shot a look at my uncle, the kind that asked what he was playing at, calling me 'Manjit' and talking about some wife who he knew I didn't want.

'Imagine that,' laughed Aunt Harpal, 'a Punjabi man making food for his wife. How can that be?'

I looked at Uncle Jag again. I wanted an explanation.

34 **to waver** [ˈweɪvə] to become unsteady

'Don't worry, Manny,' he explained in English. 'Paratha are part of the master plan.'

'What? How can a few chapatis be a part of the plan? What am I going to do? *Fly* home on one?'

'Look at you two *goreh*,' laughed my aunt. 'Speaking in your foreign language so that I cannot understand you.'

'Let me show him how to make paratha and then you will understand,' replied Uncle Jag before winking at me and telling me that he would explain it all later.

I gave both of them an odd look and walked back towards Onkar's master class in tractor-engine cleaning.

Everyone else had gone to bed by the time that I went up on to the roof with Uncle Jag and Inderjit. It was pitch black and there was a cool breeze blowing across the fields and over the village rooftops. I had become used to the darkness at night; the village had no street lights or neon signs for takeaway kebabs and burgers, not like in Leicester.

'Tomorrow I need you to pick something up for me,' Jag said in English, which meant that Inderjit was not supposed to understand what we were talking about.

'Pick up what?' I asked.

Inderjit was standing next to me. 'What are you talking about?' he asked in Punjabi, wanting the loop to extend so that it included him.

'Inderjit, he can't understand Punjabi in the same way that you can. Sometimes I have to explain things to the *gorah* in English,' said Uncle Jag, bringing a knowing smile to Inderjit's face. As far as he was concerned he had one up on me now.

'So clever, these *goreh*,' he said, mocking me. 'What do they really know, heh, Uncle-ji?'

'Yes, that's right,' assured Uncle Jag in Punjabi. And then to me in English. 'Something from Mohan. In the haveli after he has finished in the fields.'

'What am I picking up?'

'Don't worry about that. Just do what Mohan tells you,' he said, dismissing my curiosity.

'Where are you going to be?'

'Jullundur. Picking something up.'

'Why can't I come with you?' I asked.

Uncle Jag shook his head. 'I need you to be here,' he said.

'Why?'

'You ask too many questions for a *real* Punjabi man,' he said, imitating my old man. 'Listen, I'll tell you all about it, I promise. For now just do me these two favours. Pick up the package from Mohan and then get together everything that you want to take back to England with you. And don't let anyone see you get your things together. Not even the kids.'

That killed my further questions. Dead. I beamed at him, pure Cheshire Cat style. Ear to ear. My head started to spin and my heartbeat was pounding out a drum and bass tune. We were going to do it. *Really* going to do it. Get the hell out of Adumpur and India.

'Now let's get downstairs,' said Uncle Jag, in Punjabi for Inderjit.

I followed Inderjit down the stairs, smiling all the way and fell asleep clicking my heels together. I mean, there really is no place like the one that you call home.

Chapter Twenty-five
September

I sat in the haveli the following afternoon, waiting for Mohan to come in from the fields with his mysterious package. The rain had come down in sheets during the morning, stopping just after midday and it was now really hot and humid. The heat of the sun had dried out the dirt tracks and dusty yards by the time I had walked the short distance to the haveli with a bottle of cola and my camera.

I'd managed to get all my things together without anyone seeing me, packing my clothes tightly into my backpack and leaving some of the stuff I wasn't taking back with me, like T-shirts and a few pairs of shorts, lying around in the room where I'd been sleeping. My notebooks were also packed, but my personal stereo was too far gone to take. It would make a good decoy. I left it lying on the manjah that I had been using as a bed along with a few cassettes, their tape warped by the heat. The stereo had been a kind of lifeline during my first few weeks in India, drowning out my new surroundings and keeping me in touch with my real life. On the return trip I was going to be way too hyped to want to block it all out. I was going to savour it all – the trip to Delhi, the plane journey, the train or bus back

---

30 **decoy** trap – 31 **warped** [wɔːpt] bent, twisted, out of shape – 35 **way too hyped** *(inf)* far too excited – 35 **to savour** ['seɪvə] to enjoy slowly

to Leicester. Back to life, back to reality – like that Soul II Soul tune.

I'd been waiting for about an hour when Mohan rode into the yard on Inderjit's rusty bike, a cloth bag strapped across his back.

'Here is your little present,' he said, parking his bike and handing me a brown paper package about the size of two matchboxes stuck together. I got up off the hammock and took it from him, turning it over in my hands. What was it? Mohan was shaking his head at me. 'Do not even ask me, Manny. I cannot tell you or I will lose the only friend that I have in your family.'

'I'm your friend too,' I said, suddenly feeling as though I had to prove myself to him. I suppose I didn't want him to lump me in with the rest of my family. In my mind I was as much of an outsider as Uncle Jag. My family just didn't know it yet. I turned to the hammock and picked up my camera, my own little present for Mohan. 'Here. This is for you.'

Mohan looked at the camera and the two spare rolls of film that I pulled out of my pocket and shook his head. 'No, Manny-ji, no. This does not make our friendship.'

'It's not about that,' I answered defensively. 'I *want* you to have it.'

'But I don't know about these things,' he said, gesturing at the camera. His eyes were fixed on mine.

'That's not a problem, Uncle-ji.' It was only the second time that I had addressed him in that way, using 'uncle-ji'. Because he was from a lower caste than me, by tradition, I wasn't supposed to be as respectful towards him as I was with members of the same caste. I think that the combination of my present and my unintentional show of respect was what caused Mohan's eyes to fill with tears.

'Manny, I do not know what to say.'

'You don't have to say anything. It's yours. For all of the kindness you have shown me.'

'Beteh, you are truly your uncle's twin,' he said, touching the camera to his chest, over his heart. 'Here, where it counts.'

I suddenly felt kind of embarrassed because I wasn't used to displays of emotion like that. I had to change the subject. 'I'll show you how it works.'

14 **to lump sb in** *(inf)* to put sb into the same category

'Thank you, Manny,' replied Mohan, wiping his eyes and then giving me a hug. 'Give the package to your uncle when he returns from Jullundur.'

'Have you finished all your work for today? Out in the fields?'

'Yes. I was about to go home. I have a few more things to organize for you and your uncle.'

'Good,' I said, smiling. 'I'll come with you and show you how to use the camera. So that you can have pictures of your family to show *me*. Next time I come to Adumpur.'

Mohan thought for a moment, his forehead creasing. 'And they won't mind, your family, if you leave such an expensive thing with this old monkey?'

I laughed at him and punched him on the arm. 'Uncle-ji, if anyone was born to have tails, it is my family. Not you and yours.'

That seemed to kill any doubts that Mohan had about accepting my gift because he chuckled to himself all the way back to his house.

Uncle Jag beamed at me when I handed him my package later that evening. He studied it for a moment and then tucked it into his shirt pocket. We were standing in the haveli yard, by one of the storage rooms. I was tempted to ask him about the contents of the package but he cut my questions dead by handing me a large grey hessian sack.

'Here, take this,' he said in English.

I held the sack open and looked inside. It smelt damp and musty. 'What's it for?'

'It's for your things. Anything that you are taking back with you,' he replied.

My stomach flipped over with nerves and excitement and I wondered if this was what it felt like just before taking the final kick in a penalty shoot-out – half of your brain about to explode with excitement and the other half looking for a door to hide behind.

'When you get back to the house I'm going to fill another one of these sacks with the kindling that your aunts use to start the fires for cooking. You need to put your things in the bottom of your sack and then fill it up too.'

'OK.' I nodded.

---

17 to chuckle [ˈtʃʌkl] to laugh quietly – **25 hessian** thick, rough fabric – **37 kindling** small sticks used to get a fire going

'After you've done that, bring both of the sacks here. Get Inderjit to help you. Put them in the storeroom. And make sure that Inderjit doesn't see what you have in your sack.'

'No problem, Jag.' I was getting excited now. After waiting and hoping and praying for so long, my last night in Adumpur was finally here, along with butterflies in my stomach and a roller-coaster in my head. After tonight, I thought to myself, I'm gonna be on the final stretch. Home run. In my imaginary penalty shoot-out I blasted my kick high into the roof of the net, leaving the keeper bewildered and looking like shit.

We walked back to the house to find everyone gathered out in the yard doing their usual, everyday things. My older uncles were sitting drinking beer and talking about the lack of rain and how it might affect the crops. My aunts were busy chopping onions over by the outdoor stove whilst their daughters-in-law and Naseebo cooked the dinner and gossiped about the neighbours. Avtar and Rana, my eldest cousins, were still working away, and weren't due back for another month or so. Lal, Onkar and Jasbir were tending to the water buffalo and Inderjit was sitting on the tractor which was always parked near the gateway to the yard. He had Rana's kids, Ranjit and Harjit, with him as he pretended that they were on a plane, flying to America or England, or Australia. Avtar's three kids were all asleep on one manjah on the veranda. All in all it was a typical evening in Adumpur except for the fact that it was my last one, probably for a very long time.

Knowing that I'd be on a plane back to England soon made me look at my surroundings that much more closely. For the past few weeks I had spent each evening waiting for my family to go to bed so that I could sneak up on to the roof with Inderjit and Uncle Jag. Now that it was my last night I paid closer attention to the way that my aunts sat on the floor slicing onions in their hands, using knives so sharp that one slip would be enough to remove a finger or thumb. The way that my uncles sat cross-legged on their manjeh, gulping down beer and watching everyone else around them as they had yet another variation of the same conversation that they had every evening, flicking away flies from their faces every now and then. I watched Sukbir and Jaswant talking in whispers and making eye movements to emphasize each point, all the while rolling out chapatis and cooking them, or taking turns to stir a heavy steel pan that contained lentil dhal. Rajvir, cousin Lal's wife, looking as though

---

10 **bewildered** confused – 16 **to gossip** to talk about other people behind their backs – 18 **due** [dju:] expected – 42 **dhal** [dɑ:l] lentil soup

she might give birth any minute, threw little bits of kindling onto the fire as she gossiped along with them. And Balbir, cousin Onkar's wife, stood watching them, one hand leaning against a support pillar on the veranda, the other on her hip.

I watched as my cousins – all three of them barefoot – cleaned out the area where the water buffalo were tied, walking around in a sludge of water, dirt and manure with a greenish-brown tinge, the hard skin around their heels covered in the slimy mixture as they threw buckets of water over the buffalo and over each other. And Inderjit, feet dangling by the side of the tractor, one hand on the steering-wheel as he told Ranjit and Harjit his story, winking at them every so often in the way that he always did when he thought that he was telling you something mega-important. The two kids squealed in delight. Behind them, all along the veranda, flies flitted and buzzed about and the lizards began to gather on the peeling, cracked walls ready for the darkness of the village night.

Just before it got dark Inderjit helped me to carry the two sacks down to the haveli. There were no lights at all and a couple of times I stumbled as I caught my feet in the potholes that covered the track. A goat wandered part of the way with us, its eyes glowing in the dark. We left the sacks just inside the storage-room door and then padlocked it shut before heading back to the house. Inderjit hadn't asked me why we were taking so much kindling to the haveli, although I had a feeling that he would. Uncle Jag had made up some story about burning some rubbish from the fields and no-one at the house had given me a second look as I had ducked inside to retrieve my backpack, empty sack in hand. They had been too busy listening to a joke that Uncle Jag was telling them about a man who had fallen asleep in the fields after drinking home-made alcohol by mistake. My head was full of just one single thought. Home.

'So *bhai-ji*, what are all the sacks for?' Inderjit asked me, winking, as we walked back to the house.

'Nothing. Uncle-ji needs them tomorrow. To burn some rubbish.'

'Rubbish like you are telling me now?' he replied, grinning.

I looked at him and then down at my knackered Air Max. I shook my head before I spoke, then winked. 'You ask too many questions.'

---

7 sludge [slʌdʒ] soft, wet dirt – **7 manure** [məˈnjʊə] animal waste used to make crops grow – 8 **tinge** a slight colouring – 28 **to retrieve** to pick up, to get again

'So they are not for burning rubbish?'

'No, Inderjit.' I cracked a smile. 'I am going to run away back to England tomorrow and the sacks are to hide my belongings in.'

He looked at me, his mouth wide open, bewildered. I could tell what was going through his mind as he thought about what I'd said. Is he lying or is he telling the truth? I smiled wider and then broke into laughter. Inderjit waited for a few moments and then joined in my laughter, putting his hand on my shoulder.

'You know, *bhai-ji*, I really thought that you were being serious for a minute.'

'Yeah, you nearly believed me,' I teased.

'You cannot make a fool of me so easily,' he smiled, falling for my trick.

'I'll tell you the big secret tomorrow,' I told him. 'Maybe you can help.' I winked again as Inderjit nodded eagerly. Reverse psychology, Ady used to call it. 'Make a man so confused,' he once told me, 'you can tell a man anything an' he will refuse to believe it. Even the truth.' I smiled as I thought about seeing Ady again, leading Inderjit into the house with a bounce in my step.

Inside, Uncle Jag was waiting for me. He cracked open a bottle of beer for me and began telling me the next steps in the plan, in English again so that Inderjit wouldn't understand. I had assumed that we were going to get up earlier than the rest of the family so that we could escape, but my uncle told me that we would need a good start on them. As long as they didn't realize we had gone until after lunch-time, they would have to wait until the following day to follow us, by which time we would be in Delhi. Too late.

'You see, they will have to hire a car to come after us and that means going to Jullundur. No taxi-driver will agree to leave for Delhi in the afternoon, not unless you pay them in pounds or dollars,' Jag told me. 'So we need to make sure that they won't be able to work it out until the afternoon. Lunch-time at the earliest.'

'How are we going to do that?'

'We are going to make them paratha first thing in the morning. I've already told them.'

'You're going on about paratha again. How are they going to help?' Man, I was confused. What was going to happen? They were gonna be *so* full of food that they wouldn't be *able* to move? The whole thing just didn't make sense.

13 **to fall for a trick** to believe the trick (*darauf hereinfallen*)

Uncle Jag just laughed at my creased forehead and raised eyebrows. 'Leave the rest of it to me,' he said. 'You just make sure that you are ready to go when I wake you up.'

'No problem.' I was going to be awake all night anyway – wondering what on earth paratha had to do with helping me to get there.

'Good. And Manny...?' he began.

'Yeah?'

'That was really nice, what you did earlier. Giving your camera to Mohan.'

'Oh, did he tell you?' I replied.

'Tell me? That was all he talked about.'

'He told me that you were his only friend in the family. Is that true?'

'Is that what he said? I don't know. Probably.'

'What about the rest of them?'

'Well, Mohan's family has always worked for ours and everyone else treats him like a servant. They don't really talk to him or have him round socially. It's always about work.'

'But not you?'

'No, not me. Mohan has always been the only one that I talk to when I come back here. Now there's you too, of course. But Mohan's always listened to me, since I was about your age. He's been more family to me than your father or the other two. So a few years ago I gave him some fields that I don't use. He looks after them.'

'For you?'

'Yes, in a way. I'm never going to use those fields and I've no intention of settling down here, so I pretend to lease them to Mohan.'

'Pretend?' Man, the plot was thickening.

'To the family. They went mad when I told them.'

'Is that what all that stuff was about? My old man yelling down the phone when I was a kid?' I took a swig of beer and listened intently.

'Yes. I bought the family some new land which was better for crops and suchlike. And because I wasn't going to use the old land, or at least my share of it, I signed it over to Mohan.'

'Pretending that you'd only leased it?'

'Yes. Mohan is actually the proud owner of two fields which he can use for himself. Of course he pretends that he's working

---

1 **creased** [kri:st] lined

it on my behalf but actually it's his. Mohan deserves something from us, after all that his family has given to us over the years.'

'Yeah,' I nodded in agreement. 'It's not fair that everyone else treats him like a servant.'

'It's the way things are over here, Manny. People like Mohan have to work all day long just to be able to afford the most basic food. And our family gets rich off the back of his hard work. Not many people try to change things.'

'Apart from you,' I said smiling.

'And now you, too. Every little thing helps. As Mohan is fond of saying, we are all monkeys, Manny.'

'We just ain't got tails, that's all,' I said. Both of us burst into a fit of laughter and a confused-looking Inderjit looked at us both and then at the bottles of beer that we held.

'How many bottles have you had to drink?' he asked in Punjabi.

'Never mind,' replied Uncle Jag, still smiling.

'You foreigners are very strange people,' said Inderjit. 'Wearing your funny clothes and speaking your funny language. Laughing at nothing. Like monkeys.'

'Just you wait and see,' laughed Jag in Punjabi. 'We get much worse.' With that he tapped his breast pocket, where the mystery package was hidden and winked at me, imitating Inderjit.

Chapter Twenty-six
September

The darkness in the yard was broken by an overhead light on the veranda, one which Uncle Jag had turned on waking me up. I'd groaned a couple of times when he shook my shoulder before realizing suddenly the importance of the new day. Once that had dawned, I shot out of bed, showered and threw on my clothes. Outside Jag had a fire started under the stove and was busy mixing flour, water and *dhaniya* – a herb known as 'coriander' in English – together to form the dough, or *atta*, for the paratha. I stood, watching the flames flickering underneath the flat iron pan on which the paratha would be baked, the thavah. Beside the fire a pile of steel trays and bowls waited for me. Jag gestured at them.

'There's a container of fresh yogurt just inside the indoor kitchen. Go and get it and bring out a ladle too. I want to mix

37 **ladle** ['leɪdl] a large, deep spoon

some more *dhaniya* into it, ready to serve with some chopped onions, tomatoes and cucumber. They're in the fridge; bring those out too.' He spoke quietly and I wondered out loud what time it actually was. When he told me that it was just before three in the morning, I began to wish that I had never asked. I yawned and tried to wipe the tiredness from my eyes.

'Boy, I'm glad to be getting out of here. I can't handle many more of these early mornings.' It was so true, man. During my stay in Adumpur I had been getting woken up by Inderjit at around five each morning. That was like torture to me. I hadn't realized that everyone else had already been up for an hour or two before me. Sack that. Not me, dread. When I got back to Leicester I was going to make it a priority to get in a solid month or two of lie-ins.

I headed wearily for the indoor kitchen, where I found the yoghurt, ladle and chopped vegetables. I took them back out to the yard where I found Jag standing over a large pan of buffalo milk, watching it come to the boil so he could make some tea. 'So what's the plan?' I asked him in English.

He pointed towards the indoor kitchen. 'All the adults, including Jasbir and Inderjit, will be eating paratha. They're not for the kids; they don't really like them anyway so I've bought them some egg noodles and ketchup. Or they can have fried bread with jam. I need you to sort them out when they get up.'

'No problem,' I said as I watched my uncle roll out the paratha and pass them to me to bake on the *thavah*.

We served up breakfast around quarter to four by which time it had been light for a while. Uncle Jag took care of the adults while I gave the kids platefuls of noodles and ketchup. The food seemed to go down quite well and everyone, my older uncles included, congratulated us on how nice it was. As the cooks, of course, we simply served the food but didn't eat any ourselves so, by the time everyone else had finished eating, my stomach had begun to growl. Jag fried up some slices of bread for us and I ate them loaded with strawberry-flavoured jam.

By half past four, everyone had gone off to their various chores and the courtyard was deserted except for my uncle and myself. Jag came over to me and pulled me by the arm.

'Go over to the haveli and get your things. I'll meet you by the front gate in five minutes. Mohan will have a car waiting for us.'

---

15 **weary** ['wɪəri] very tired

My heart jumped into my mouth. It was actually happening. We were actually on our way. I took a last look around the courtyard, realizing that I wasn't going to miss the place at all. I felt like a prisoner waiting at the prison gates, my last moments of captivity before I was set free. I wiped my forehead and then headed for the haveli at full pelt, dodging the old goat that lived on the path and jumping over the potholes. I was so excited that I emptied the kindling from the sack out in the haveli yard, grabbing my backpack before heading back to the front of the house. Mohan was standing there with a man who looked just like him, only younger. Behind them was a small white car that looked a bit like a Ford Fiesta, but more box-shaped. I went over to give Mohan a hug.

'So, you are actually going?' smiled Mohan as I stepped back.

'Yes, Uncle-ji.'

'Will you miss this old monkey when you are back in your foreign home with all your foreign things?'

'Of course I will. Just don't go growing any tails, OK?'

Mohan gave me a big smile, then introduced me to his nephew, Bahadur, who was going to drive us to Delhi. He opened the back for me and I put my backpack in as Jag came out. Throwing a travel bag into the car, he ushered me in then turned and shook hands with Mohan. They exchanged a few words and then the car was moving. We were off, through the narrow streets of Adumpur, across to the other side of the village and out onto the main road! It all happened so quickly that I didn't even have time to register it all. One minute we were outside the house and the next travelling along a wide road, the driver dodging between the usual other cars, buses, trucks, pedestrians and animals. I yawned deeply and fell asleep, my head resting against the rear side window, as I listened to Jag and Bahadur talking; still wondering about how we had managed to get out of the house without being seen. Or why the family wouldn't immediately notice my absence.

Chapter Twenty-seven
September

'I can't believe that you gave them weed, man! That's just mad.'

'Only enough to send them to sleep for a few hours. It won't hurt them.'

---

5 **captivity** imprisonment – 6 **at full pelt** at full speed, very fast – 22 **to usher** [ˈʌʃə] to bring in (especially by showing the way)

'Yeah, but weed? No wonder you wanted the kids to eat something else. Man, they're gonna be vexed when they wake up.'

'At least the kids were OK. I left them with Naseebo. No harm done. Well, not much.'

I had woken up about half an hour after we had left Adumpur when the car had braked sharply to avoid hitting a bull in the middle of the road. The first thing I had asked Jag was how we managed to escape without the rest of the family noticing. He had told the family that he was taking me on a trip to Jalandhar for the day. I hadn't expected him to tell me that the herbs that had been mixed into the yoghurt and those that went into the paratha had been weed. Marijuana. My mouth just fell open. For a good minute. And then I creased up with laughter, so much that my eyes started to water and my ribcage began to ache. Weed! I couldn't believe that in all my excitement I hadn't recognized the herb for what it was. And no wonder Mohan hadn't wanted to tell me what was in the mysterious package.

I was trying to imagine Uncle Piara after he woke up, suffering from the 'munchies' and wondering what the hell had happened to him. It was like something out of an Eddie Murphy movie. Jag just grinned at me when he told me. Like it was no big deal. He told me that there was no way that they would find out. He had brought the rest of the stuff with him, ditching it by the road as we left Jullundur. There was probably some poor goat wandering through the streets, high as a kite, wondering where it was going and what was happening to it. The very thought of it made me laugh even harder. Ordinarily, I would have been bricking myself, worried that I was gonna get murdered by my old man for pulling such a stunt, but I figured that it was just what they deserved for keeping me prisoner for so long. As Ady always liked to say – 'One in yer eye, boss.'

We arrived in Delhi in the late afternoon and immediately the traffic worsened all around us. The roads were absolute chaos with trucks, cars, scooters, carts and motorized three-wheelers weaving in and out and around each other whilst people on foot crossed into the path of oncoming traffic, not looking where they were going, as though they were wearing suits of armour. Added to the chaos were more people pedalling along on rusty bikes, three and sometimes four to a frame and the usual assortment

---

2 **vexed** [vekst] angry, annoyed displeased – 15 **ribcage** the structure of ribs in your chest – 20 **the munchies** ['mʌntʃɪz] *(inf, here)* hunger, feeling the strong urge to eat, which often happens after using marijuana – 24 **to ditch** to throw out (into the ditch) – 38 **armour** ['ɑːmə] metal protection worn in battle – 40 **assortment** variety

of cows, bulls, goats, pigs and stray dogs. Man, it was so crazy that I started to feel claustrophobic, sitting in all that traffic, watching everything going on around me.

Bahadur parked up right outside our destination, the British Airways ticket office in downtown Delhi, and Jag told me that we were going to pick up the tickets and then head straight for the airport, Indira Gandhi International, which was about twelve miles or so outside of the centre. He had booked me onto a flight leaving at two the following morning, enough time to get some food and have a quick look around Delhi.

But it didn't go completely smoothly. When we found the queue in the ticket office, we saw that the clerk at the front was shaking his head, as if to say sorry.

'What do you reckon is going on, Uncle-ji ... er, I mean, Jag?'

'Looks like there's some kind of delay, Manny. Hang on, I'll go and find out.' He returned after about five minutes with the bad news. 'First available flight will probably be tomorrow night, around midnight.'

I shrugged. 'Airport better be comfortable,' I said, taking my passport and ticket from Jag and putting them into my bag.

Jag shook his head. 'Two rooms at the Metro,' he said. 'Booked and ready.'

'The Metro?' I asked, wondering where that was.

'My favourite hotel in Delhi,' replied Jag, smiling.

'To the Metro it is then,' I said, smiling back at him.

Chapter Twenty-eight
September

We had lunch the following day at a restaurant called 'Croissants Etc' on Connaught Place in the heart of Delhi. I had been amazed to find out that you could buy something like a croissant in India at all. Earlier we had taken a walk around the centre of Delhi. It was just like being at home. I saw an Odeon cinema, an American Express bureau, a Thomas Cook travel agents, and loads of trendy looking restaurants and delis called 'Zen' and 'Rodeo' – another world compared to the one that I had been used to in Adumpur and Jullundur. Jag told me that Delhi was more cosmopolitan than the rest of India. The major

---

35 **cosmopolitan** international, multi-ethnic (city)

cities in India – Delhi and Mumbai – were more modern than the rest. They were like the financial and media centres of India, a bit like London and Manchester are in England. Because of that there was more money and more commercial outlets like the restaurants and bars that he showed me. My whole image of India needed upgrading – like buying the latest version of your favourite computer game because the old one just doesn't cut it any more.

'Will you give me your address so that I can write to you?' I had just finished my lunch and was sitting staring out of the window.

'Yes, of course I will. I want to know all about what you decide to do with your arranged marriage.'

I still didn't know how it was all going to work out. I knew that I didn't want this marriage. That I couldn't live my life like that, in that traditional way. But as for what I was going to *do* about it, that was something that I needed to think about, get sorted out. Talking to Jag made me realize that I was going to have to make a big decision soon. A straight choice between my family and my freedom. The only question was whether it was going to be too big. For I would be cut off from my family if I chose freedom. On my own. And that would be a high price to pay.

Jag seemed to know what was going on in my head because he pushed aside his plate and answered the question for me. 'Everything you decide on in your life has a cost, Manny.'

'How do you mean?'

'Well, take this whole marriage thing. I know that you're going to have all these doubts in your mind about whether you are doing the right thing or not.'

'Definitely.'

'What you've got to ask yourself is what *you* want out of life. At the end of the day it's about you being happy doing what *you* want. Or keeping your parents happy by doing what *they* say.'

'I know, Jag. The thing is, it's really hard. I mean if I don't go through with it they're going to disown me.'

'Like they did with me, you mean?'

'No, because they still talk to you and you visit them all the time. I'm talking about being totally cut off. That's what they'll do.'

'And that might be too high a price to pay?'

'Yeah.'

35 **to disown** to reject so that you are no more a member of the family

'Straight choice?'

'Totally. And if I do end up doing what I want to, I'm just going to feel like the most selfish person on the planet.'

'Trying to achieve your goals doesn't make you selfish. Ask yourself this, Manny. In five years from now, where do you see yourself? Tied down to a wife and house that you don't want or doing all those things that you told me about when I first met you? You know, getting an education, travelling. Becoming a writer or whatever.'

He was right. I couldn't see myself doing that whole family thing. I mean I didn't know what I was actually going to be doing in five years' time, but it was going to have to be something that I decided on and not my parents. I was too young to just lie down and let my whole life be mapped out by someone else. And Jag was like the perfect role model. He had escaped all that traditional shit and he wasn't doing too badly. He wasn't the junkie dropout that my old man had told me I'd become if I didn't do the 'honourable' thing and marry some girl who I didn't even know. He wasn't living on the streets or in prison. He just had a life that he wanted. Not one that had been created for him by someone else. No, Jag was right. Making your own decisions about life didn't mean that you were selfish. Not at all.

Back at the hotel that night I packed all my things together, finding space in my backpack for presents that I had bought for Ady and Lisa. For Ady, I'd found a Cypress Hill CD that I knew he didn't have (at least he *hadn't* had it the last time I saw him) which had only cost me the same as about three English pounds. Lisa was different and I didn't know what to get her. In the end I settled for a set of three fat Buddha candles and a cat carved out of sandalwood, because I knew that she loved cats. I hadn't found a present for Jag though I felt that I should, after all the help he'd given me. In the end I told him this.

'Manny, you don't have to buy me anything. I'm not a kid.'

'Yeah, but after all you've done for me...'

'Just your company is enough. In a way I'm glad that you are going through all this arranged marriage thing. I was beginning to think that I was a one-off in this family.'

'I don't get you.'

'Sometimes, even now, after all this time, I feel guilty and selfish and all those things myself. When you told me about how the rest of the family have treated you, that reminded me of the

---

4 **to achieve** to attain, fulfil – 26 **Cypress Hill** ['saiprəs] Latin American hip hop group from California

reasons why I did what I did. And talking to you, well, that made me realize why I left the whole family set-up. That my reasons for not following their traditions weren't selfish at all. They were just the right decisions for me and my life.'

'But you still feel guilty sometimes?'

'Yes, for about a minute – then I start to think about all the good things that I have in my life and I stop feeling so bad.'

'So are you like married or whatever? Aunt Harpal told me a load of rumours about you when we first met, about having a wife and kids somewhere.' As I finished speaking, Jag looked at me with a raised eyebrow and then smiled.

'Not a wife, a girlfriend, Nancy. She's a lawyer in Sydney. And Mia.'

'Who's Mia?' I asked as Jag pulled out his wallet to show me a picture of a pretty blond woman and a kid who must have been about four or five.

'My daughter. Your cousin.'

I was well shocked. 'How come you didn't tell me before, you know, when I was asking you all those stupid questions and that?'

'You never asked.' He was right too. I hadn't asked him although I had been wondering about it. Every time he talked about his life he got this half-sad, half-happy look in his eyes. I guessed it was because he missed his family when he was away from them. His real family.

'You must miss them when you're away?'

'Yes I do. But you see, Manny, that's what I'm talking about. I could have done all of that traditional stuff but it just wasn't for me. And if I had, I never would have met Nancy and we wouldn't have had such a beautiful daughter.'

I stared at the photo in my hand.

'Keep it, kiddo,' Jag said. 'I've got another one. Besides, I want you to know about my family, so that you'll know them when you come to visit.'

'I will, Jag. I promise. I just can't believe that you have a kid and that.'

'Most of the time, Manny, neither can I.'

The rest of the night flew by in a kind of haze. Jag and I had quite a few drinks in the hotel bar before leaving for the airport. We

---

9 **rumour** information (often untrue) about sth or sb that is passed on from person to person – 38 **haze** fog, mist

had swapped addresses – I gave him Ady's brother's, knowing that Ady wouldn't mind. After all, by the time that I had finished my cheat, who knew where I would be living. The nearer it got to departure time, the more I began worrying about what kind of reception I was going to get from my old man and my brothers. I mean, I wasn't expecting them to be happy about my return. They'd be fuming about my escape from the village, assuming my uncles had told them – in fact, they'd probably sent a telegram to my old man, followed up with several phone calls, all reverse charged, to make *sure* he knew.

At the airport everything ran smoothly and I entered the departure lounge about half past two, after saying goodbye to Jag and thanking him for all his help. Doing that made me sad too, and I had to fight back tears at one point. Not that I was going to cry in front of him, no way, man. But you know when you get that feeling – that lump in your throat? That was what was going on. I just wasn't used to being treated like I was important, like I mattered, and that's what Jag did. Treated me like a human being. Like an adult.

I was so tired that I fell asleep on the plane and got woken up about six hours into the flight by a really pretty stewardess. I had about three cups of coffee and a bar of chocolate and then sat and watched all the other passengers as the plane took me home. A few hours later, I was standing in Heathrow, and after that everything just flew by – the tube, the station, the train to Leicester, and then the familiar number 22 bus. It came up outside Leicester station like a best mate, just as I got to the bus stop, my legs aching and my head pounding. Now I was only fifteen minutes away from another confrontation with my family.

As I sat on the top deck of the bus, smoking my duty-free cigarettes, looking down at all the familiar shops and restaurants, my stomach was turning over, even though I was happy to be home. I thought about doing a runner as the bus passed the junction of Evington and St Stephen's Road, comforted because Ady was living just a few minutes from there with his brother. Only running was too easy. I had to go home and face the music. And the time had come to move my cheat up to the final level and blow up the mothership.

---

1 **to swap** to exchange – 10 **reverse charged** the person who is called has to pay for the phone call *(R-Gespräch)* – 25 **tube** London underground railway system

The bus took a left on to Evington Drive, and then it was too late. I was one bus stop from my house. From my family. I rang the bell, picked up my bag and stumbled down the aisle, and then down the stairs as the bus pulled up outside my house. My dad's car was on the drive and I walked around it, up to the door and rang the doorbell. The bell played some dodgy tune for about thirty seconds and then the door opened and I stood face to face with Ranjit. I looked up at him and smiled, wondering what he was going to say, how he was going to react. But he just glared at me and then turned back into the hall. I waited a moment, thinking about heading back up to Ady's house, before following him in. As I reached the doorway to the living room, my old man came out.

'So, you have arrived then, Manjit?' he asked me in Punjabi. Then he slapped me across the back of the head with his huge hand, sending me crashing into the side of the stairway. My head stung and, as I turned to complain, to shout, to cry, he punched me full in the face.

3 **aisle** [aɪl] gangway

part four

the wedding

Chapter Twenty-nine
October

'Bwoi, you look darker than me y'know.' Ady sat in his brother's house in Highfields, drinking from a can of Red Stripe. I just grinned at him before moving my neck from side to side, trying to relax. It was the middle of October, I'd been back over a month now and I was on a night off from work.

I was working night shifts with Ady in a supermarket warehouse up in Oadby. The job was basically shit – one of those training scheme things for school leavers. All I did was load and unload boxes of tinned beans and stuff, but the money was all right and I got to see Ady all the time in his new role as father to his son, Zachariah. It also meant that I didn't have to spend any time with my family and I could save up the money to move out and get my own place, even though, as far as my family were concerned, I was still getting married at the end of November. That was fine with me. I was going to let them carry on thinking just that, and then do a runner about a week before the actual day of the wedding. Revenge. Pure and simple.

The beating that I got on my return had only made me stronger, more determined to go my own way. I hadn't really thought that my old man would welcome me back with open arms, but I certainly hadn't expected to get beaten like that and then locked up in my room for two whole days. Harry, the wanker, had even gone and fitted a new lock on my bedroom door just so that they could keep me prisoner. Man, I felt like a character from one of those documentaries about arranged marriages, the ones where the parents have hired taxi-drivers to find their kids and bring them back. The victims in those things always seem to be women, though – young girls – yet here I was, nearly seventeen and a bloke, and I was getting the same shit done to me.

I was so angry and hurt that I couldn't even look at Harry or my old man without wanting to hit them. And my mum had just carried on as before, ignoring me until it was time to lay on the emotional blackmail, thick like butter. Slapping her thighs and asking the Lord to help me. It was coming at me from all directions – the threats, the punches, the softly-softly approach that Ranjit and Jas began to use, telling me that it wouldn't be so bad. That I'd get used to it, settle down, grow with all my new responsibilities. It was mental torture. And that's why my job was such a godsend.

The other good thing about the job was that my family thought I was finally beginning to sort myself out by doing it. Even though I was angry with them and hardly spoke to them, I think that they thought I was accepting my fate because I hadn't done a runner and I hadn't said that I wasn't going to get married. I hadn't said that I was going to either, but my old man and Harry were so arrogant that they thought everything was hunky-dory, just because I had stopped complaining. Ranjit and Jas were the only ones who tried to talk to me, and both of them apologized for my being left in India, even though they had had nothing to do with it. As far as my old man was concerned I was working hard and saving money – just what he had always wanted for me *and* without needing an education. I was – only on the nights when I had loads of 'overtime' to do, I'd go and chill out with Ady, Sarah and Zac, or go to a bar or club. When they thought I was busy stacking shelves, I was actually out drinking and smoking weed and hatching a plan to get back at them. Or sitting in Ady's living room playing on his brother's Playstation and making faces at Zac who had the most amazing grin I'd ever seen. He was the spitting image of his dad.

'So you got Saturday night off then?' said Ady as I lit myself a spliff.

'Yeah, but I'm gonna have to work Monday night to make up for it.'

'What, they can't just give you the night off?'

'Yeah, they can, but I need the money if I'm gonna make my plan work.'

'So you definitely doing it, yeah?' Ady shouldn't have had to wait for my reply. He should have known what I was going to say.

'Definitely, one hundred an' fifty per cent, sure as goddamit I am, bwoi.'

'Man, that's the worst mix of accents I've ever heard, mofo. What was that? US rap star meets hick-town sheriff meets yardie?' He shook his head and smiled.

---

11 **hunky-dory** *(inf)* okay, fine – 20 **to hatch a plan** to make a well thought-out plan *(ausbrüten)* – 23 **to be the spitting image of sb** to look exactly like – 37 **hick-town** *(inf)* small village – 38 **yardie** ['jɑːdi] member of a violent criminal organization especially involved in drug-dealing

'I've got to do it, Ady. For me. Man, I can't live the way they want me to. Can you see me with a wife at seventeen? That's just lame.'

'Well, look at me, with a kid at my age. And Sarah may as well be my wife for all the nagging she does. Anyway, I spoke to Steve an' he's cool about you staying here for a while, but you're gonna have to sleep on the sofa, man, and, believe me, that thing is about as comfy as a bag of spuds, dread.' Steve, Ady's brother had told me himself that it would be OK to stay, but it was nice to hear Ady reassure me.

'Well, like Lisa always used to say, beggars can't be...'

'You seen her since you got back?'

I looked at him and shook my head. I had written to her at her parents' house but she hadn't replied. That had been two weeks ago and I was giving up hope that she'd get in touch. Then again, maybe she'd written back and Harry had stolen the letter.

Ady must have caught the flow of my thoughts because he just shook his head. 'Listen, Manny, why don't you go and find out whether she's tried to get in touch or not? Go and see her mum.'

'I keep meaning to but something stops me, like I'm too embarrassed or scared. I know I shouldn't be but I am.'

Ady thought about it for a second and then broke into a smile. 'Cool. If *you* ain't going to go see her, *she*'s going to come see you man. Jus' like Mohammed an' him mountain.'

I looked at him like he was mad. I mean, what was she going to do – turn up at my old man's door? Ady was cool and that but sometimes he didn't half talk some...

'Chill out, bredren, innit,' he said in a high-pitched voice. 'We going out Saturday night, guy, an' she's gonna come too, my dan.'

'And how you going to fix that?' I replied smiling at his piss-take of the Asian 'Jamaicans' that we saw all over Leicester.

'Easy. I'm gonna make her cousin, my girl, a nice tea when she gets in from work tomorrow...'

'Yeah all right – do it.' I was beginning to get excited and he hadn't even got Sarah to call Lisa yet.

'We'll do it as a pure surprise 'ting. She won't have a clue.'

---

5 **to nag** to always find fault with sb – 8 **comfy** [ˈkʌmfi] *(BE inf)* comfortable – 8 **spud** *(inf)* potato – 29 **bredren** brethren (old plural of 'brother'; term used to address members of a (religious) group – 29 **high-pitched** with a high tone

I spent the rest of that week working nights at the supermarket and avoiding all contact with my family. I hardly saw my old man at all, and when I did he was pissed. I was just looking forward to Saturday night, hoping that Sarah had got in touch with Lisa. Hoping that she'd turn up.

On the Friday afternoon Ranjit was at home and as I walked into the kitchen to make some tea, he stood waiting, making it obvious that he wanted to talk to me.

'We have to sort out some things about the wedding, Manjit,' he said, not looking at me. I threw a tea bag into my mug and said nothing, waiting for him to continue. The wedding was just over a month away and this was the first time that anyone had mentioned it to me directly. 'Daddy-ji has sorted out all the stuff. The hall and the food. Everything is set.'

'Great.' My answer was sarcastic but I decided that it would be best to just play along with him. See what he had to say.

He waved a piece of paper in my face and then threw it down on the worktop next to my mug. 'The whole cost of the food and the hall and everything is nearly ten thousand pounds, innit.'

'So? I never asked you to spend all that.'

'Listen. I know you are still upset about India but you got to understand, man. Daddy-ji has spent all of that for you. Not for anyone else. It's your wedding.'

'I thought it was yours.'

'Don't try to be clever, man. I'm just telling you that we are doing it for your own good. How much more does Daddy-ji have to do to show you?'

I was tempted to launch into a speech about how money wasn't important to me and all that but it would have been wasted on my oldest brother. I don't think he would have understood what I was getting at.

At this moment, Harry walked in and stood right in my face. 'You better not do anything to mess it all up, innit?' he bellowed. 'Everything is set. You better not damage our family name, Manjit, or I'm gonna damage you.'

I ignored Harry and looked past him to Ranjit. 'But I've already told you that I'll do it. Get married and that.'

'No you ain't. We've told *you* that. You better just accept it or that's it for you,' Harry butted in without giving Ranjit a chance to speak.

I continued to ignore him. 'So what you're asking me, Ranjit, is whether I'm going to say yes?'

'No, Manjit. I'm telling you that everything is ready. All you have to do is what we tell you to do. Me and Jas have taken on the responsibility, innit. I don't care what you do when you get married but you are getting married. All of our reputation, our *izzat*, depends on it.'

'So you're responsible for it all? And the old man's spent all that money?' A bulb exploded into life inside my head. An idea.

'Ain't that what I just said to you?'

'OK, I'll do it. But afterwards I'm gonna do what I want.'

'Afterwards, Manjit, you will be your own man with your own responsibility. Straight like the rest of us.' He put his hand on my shoulder.

'What?' I asked, my brain sparkling – an idea for revenge that was so sweet it could have been marketed by Cadbury's or someone. Sweet like chocolate.

'Maybe, one day,' Ranjit continued, 'you will become a real Jat. One of us. Our life ain't bad like you think it is. We are just different. Not like those *goreh*. We have to live in our own society, innit? How else our kids gonna be good Punjabis?'

I gave Ranjit half a smile when he'd finished, wondering how we could be related at all. He was like a weaker version of my old man with his simple view of the world. In a way I actually felt quite sorry for him. It was obvious that he couldn't stand up to our dad. It was like he'd been brainwashed. And I realized that underneath all that was my brother, and I didn't even really know who he was – not that I was going to let such thoughts deflect me now. My plan was forming and I had to see it through.

* * *

That Saturday night I left for work as usual, around half past six in the evening, but instead of heading for the warehouse in Oadby, I walked up Evington Road to Ady's place. Once I got there I changed into my going-out clothes: a pair of straight black trousers, black Caterpillars and a deep blue, short-sleeved shirt, all stuff that I'd bought as soon as I got back from India and lost my guilt complex about rich and poor. It was a way of

28 **to deflect** to prevent

saying to my old man that I was in charge now, and I was gonna spend my money how I wanted, on what I wanted.

Ady had got us onto the guest list of this new club just outside town, where his brother was a doorman and where the house DJ, Bump Allen, was playing. I'd heard him once before, back before I was expelled from school and he had been wicked. Normally I only listened to ragga or jungle, but Ady said that we should broaden our horizons, musically, and I was up for that, especially as it was free.

'Honeyz, man. Nuff gal,' he said as we stood by the bar in the upstairs room, trying to avoid spilling our drinks. It was heaving in there, and the air-conditioning didn't seem to be working. For a moment the temperature reminded me of being in India because my shirt was stuck to my back and my forehead was dripping with sweat. I gave Ady my beer to look after and headed through the crowd for the toilets, wanting to throw some water on my face to stop me looking like a sweaty geek – even if everyone else in the place was sweating the same way. I walked in past two girls who were giggling at each other, pissed up to a point where they thought it was clever to be in the men's toilets. One of them was wearing a see-through black dress with only a thong on underneath and the other had on a short black dress that showed off how big her tits were. I gave them a sly look on my way back towards the bar but not for too long. My mind was on Lisa, whether she was going to turn up – and what I was going to say to her if she did.

When I got back, Ady was chatting to Sarah but still eyeing up every other girl that went by. Sarah didn't look even slightly bothered by what he was doing but after so long, I suppose she was used to him playing the idiot. I knocked my beer back, then headed downstairs to the foyer area. Steve, Ady's brother, was standing just inside the door, chatting to a tall blond girl. I gave him a smile and walked outside. Around twenty people were milling about in the car park, doing the same as me. I went and sat on the car-park wall, facing the door. About ten minutes later, someone tapped me on the shoulder. I turned, expecting to see an old school friend and my eyes nearly popped out of my head.

Lisa.

'Hello stranger.'

11 **heaving** extremely crowded – 22 **thong** piece of underwear with a single string instead of a back part

I didn't even reply. Jumping off the wall, I hugged her so hard that she went red, then broke away and looked at her. She looked wicked. Her hair was a lot shorter, almost cropped to her head, and she had a really deep tan which stood out against the little white top she was wearing. I couldn't look away. I just stood there staring at her and holding her hand. And then she started to cry.

Chapter Thirty
November

Sunday nights became a regular 'overtime' slot for me at work. I'd leave the house at six and come back in at around eight the next morning, having spent the night with Lisa at her parents' house. After meeting up again that night, it was like we'd never been apart. Lisa told me that she had missed me as much as I had missed her, and that she had been worried that I might not come back from India at all. Her parents had been great, welcoming me back like a long-lost son, and telling me that I could stay whenever I wanted to. My cheat was all but planned by then and I let Lisa and her dad in on it. They were a bit shocked but still told me that I had their backing.

Having Lisa to confide in again really helped to sort my head out. I had talked to Ady about things quite a lot but Lisa had this totally different way of looking at things. She kept on telling me that I had to get out, get away from the whole marriage thing, today. *Now.* Her argument was that I didn't need to get revenge on my family. I should just tell them to leave me alone and walk out. After all, I had a job now and I was earning good money for a seventeen-year-old, enough to rent a flat. The thing is, it wasn't what Lisa said that made her so special. It was the fact that she totally believed in me, and did her best to understand my situation. She was like another version of Jag, only not as wise yet, with her 'you have to do it' attitude. There were times when I would begin to doubt what I was going to do. Was I gonna be able to just walk out on my family. How was I going to survive? All that sort of stuff. Lisa was like my straight and narrow path guide, pushing me on in the right direction. And I loved her for it. Especially as the wedding drew closer and closer.

---

3 **cropped** [krɒpt] cut very short – 19 **to confide in** to share secrets, personal thoughts and ideas

Two weeks before the actual day of the wedding, the girl's family came round on a Sunday afternoon. The girl didn't actually come with them. There were about fifteen of them, all crammed into our living room, drinking tea and eating samosas. All of them were looking at me, but not one actually spoke to me or asked me anything. I felt like some kind of prize bull surrounded by farmers eager to get their cows pregnant. They were all assuming that I was fine with the whole thing, and I let them think that way. To tell you the truth, I was past the point of caring by then. One half of me was scared and nervous, still questioning what I was doing, and the other was defiant. Man, I had the secret code. All I had to do now was type it in and the cheat would work its magic and take me on, up to the next level, past all the monsters in my way.

I just sat there, on my chair, staring down at the floor or up at the ceiling. At one point the girl's aunt made a crack about how I was shy and embarrassed which made all the women and some of the men laugh. I zoomed out of the room, out of the whole situation, until I was like a fly on the wall, looking down at what was going on, watching and studying my subjects. Anyone looking in would have seen a happy gathering of in-laws on a warm Sunday afternoon in November. Everyone was chatting and smiling, passing round food and cups of tea, and talking with excitement about the forthcoming wedding. But zoom in close and it was a different picture. My old man was sitting in a ruffled beige suit, his Sunday best, with his eyes all bloodshot and his hands shaking from a lack of booze. My supposed father-in-law looked pretty much the same as my old man, only his suit was black and he had a turban wrapped around his head. My brothers were sitting, slurping their tea and stuffing samosas into their gobs – water buffalo at feeding time. My mum was talking about how lucky we were to be such a well-off family, with such good sons. Not like the family in No. 52 whose son had run off with a white girl, or the daughter from No. 63 who married a Hindu. And then there was the Muslim family in No. 25 whose grandfather and father were in prison for smuggling heroin and weed. Me, the intended groom? I was

---

3 **crammed** close together in a small space – 4 **samosa** [sə'məʊsə] Indian food made from meat or vegetables covered in thin pastry and boiled in hot oil – 11 **defiant** [dɪ'faɪənt] bravely resisting, stubborn – 16 **crack** *(inf)* joke – 21 **gathering** a meeting, coming together in a group – 31 **gob** *(BE, inf, vul)* mouth – 37 **groom** bridegroom

being told in a low whisper by Jas to smile. Don't upset the apple cart. DON'T UPSET THE APPLE CAR...

Only the apples were rotten and I didn't want them anyway.

Later, after my 'in-laws' had gone, my old man came up to me as I was getting ready for my 'overtime'. He was carrying a wad of cash in his hands and smiling. I was in the kitchen, making myself a cheese and pickle sandwich, and, although I tried to ignore him, he came up and grabbed the back of my neck in his big, meaty hand. The smell of booze invaded my nose. So much for not drinking on Sundays I thought to myself. He must have had a couple of crafty shots when no-one had been watching.

'Good boy, ju are the good boy, Manjit,' he said in his broken, dodgy English before switching to Punjabi. 'Here, take this money and buy yourself a suit for the wedding. Get a shirt and tie too.'

'I've got all of those already,' I told him, not wanting to take his dough.

'No! You have to take it. You have done me proud, beteh.' His eyes started to well up as the booze in his blood began to make him all emotional.

'I've got a suit and all that. I don't need another one,' I said, hoping that he'd wander off and leave me alone. He didn't. He just stood there, squeezing my neck even harder, tears in his eyes.

'I remember when I got married,' he told me. 'We couldn't afford a suit so I had to borrow one from my cousin, Jit. Oh what a happy day that was. We drank so much whisky and ate so much meat. Just like you youngsters do now. The best party of your life is the day of your marriage.'

'Yeah, I'm sure it is,' I replied in English, all sarcastic, but he didn't hear me. He just kept on talking.

'You'll see. You thought that we were trying to ruin your life with this but you will see. Even after all the bad things that you have done to us, Manjit, you have still turned out to be a good Punjabi man. You'll see. Soon you will have a wife and children to look after and then you will know what I have been through, the pressure I have to face.'

I looked at him and wondered whether he was telling me all this stuff to make me feel bad or because he just wanted to get it off his chest. I had heard him say the same shit to my brothers

---

5 **wad of cash** [wɒd] a large roll of money – 17 **dough** [dəʊ] *(inf)* money

and always when he'd had a skinful to drink, like he couldn't open up unless he was so drunk that he was close to passing out. Sometimes I'd felt bad for him, wondering what made him drink so much. But there was nothing wrong with his life. He had a house and a job and all his kids had done what he wanted – apart from me. He was just a pisshead. An alcoholic. And that was no-one's fault but his own.

'Here,' he said thrusting the money into my hands. 'Take this and make me proud of you, Manjit.'

I counted the money quickly. It was around six hundred quid in twenties and tens. Realizing that he had just provided me with the last part of my cheat, I pocketed the money and said thank you, feeling bad for a minute that I had taken it, before I went back to thinking for me and not for him. After all the punches and the kicks and the beatings with sticks that I had taken from him throughout my life, not to mention all the lies and the emotional stuff, surely I was entitled to take his money, especially as it was probably going to be for the last time.

I'd explained to Ady what I had planned and what I needed him to do. He was cool about it but still wanted to know why I was going to wait for so long. Why not just walk out now? The answer was no. Right or wrong, it was something that I wanted to do. That I needed to do. I had to show them that I was different from them. An individual. That all their threats and violence and money and everything couldn't stop me being what I wanted to be. And once I had explained all of that to Ady he started to agree with me.

'Listen, Manny, do what you feel an' that, but make sure you understand. Once you do this, they're gonna want your blood.'

'I know, Ady. And I don't care. They've had enough of my blood already.'

'And you know that you'll never be able to go back.'

I looked at him and tried to smile, only I couldn't. 'Yeah. I know that this will be the end of my relationship with all of them. That's all I've thought about for the past year. For the past four years. It's too late to change it now.'

'What, definitely?' asked Ady, raising an eyebrow.

'Yeah, one hundred per cent. I'm never going to forgive them for all the shit, India and all that. Never.'

'Well in that case,' smiled Ady, 'you can count on me, boss.'

17 **to be entitled** to have the right to

'Thanks, man. It means a lot to me.'
'No problem.'
'Cool.' I looked at him and winked.
'Now,' replied Ady, winking back. 'We gonna synchronize watches or what?'

Chapter Thirty-one
Friday 28th November

'I'm gonna tidy up my room in a bit, get it all cleared up and ready.'

Harry winked at me and grinned. 'You're gonna have to get rid of all your magazines now,' he said. 'Never mind, you'll be getting plenty of the real thing soon, innit?'

'Don't be so crude, Harry,' replied Jas, acting as my protector. 'Manny isn't like you. He's a much more sensitive man.'

I let them carry on: Harry laughing at the fact that Jas had called me sensitive – not that he knew what it meant anyway; and Jas acting as my favourite sister-in-law and best friend rolled into one. I just smiled and let them get on with it, buzzing with the thought that they had all fallen for my little act and laughing inside at how easy tricking them had been. Man, they were like one hundred per cent stupid. I mean, as far as they were concerned I'd had a complete personality change – gone from being totally against getting married only a few weeks earlier, to being up for it. I had stoked the fire a bit by admitting to Jas that I was 'looking forward' to settling down, that I'd realized my duty to the family and all that shit. She had passed that on to Ranjit, who in turn had told the old man. Even my mum had come up to me earlier in the day to tell me what a wonderful son I had finally become. Easy as. And I didn't feel the slightest bit guilty for it. They only liked me again because they thought that I had caved in to all the pressure. They weren't interested in *me*, the person that I was, not if it didn't match their idea of right and wrong. The more that they were nice to me, the more I saw just how two-faced they really were. And that made me mad. It was like my old man saying, 'Hey, I know that I've kicked seven shades of shit out of you for most of your life, but look at this.

---

4 **to synchronize** [ˈsɪŋkrənaɪz] to coordinate – 22 **to stoke the fire** to heat up a situation

I'm sorry, I really am and here's a wife and lots of money to prove it.' They made me sick, all of them.

I left them to their fake joy and went upstairs to my room to 'tidy up'. Punjabi weddings are traditionally stretched out over three days, with the actual ceremony on the last of those days – and the first two days of this were today and tomorrow. It's an excuse to have a big party, although there are all these mini-ceremonies that have to be done at set times on each day. The house was full of people. Although it was still early on Friday morning, some of my uncles, aunts and cousins were beginning to arrive already, all of them congratulating me on my good luck and telling me that I was making my old man very happy, and for that I was a good son, and could I talk to so and so who was on the path to wicked ways and needed the guidance of a good Punjabi boy to straighten him out. It was a complete head trip and there would be even more people turning up tomorrow. Thing was, all the people around gave me the cover I needed to get phase one of my cheat into action. I had told Jas that there was a lot of junk in my room, lots of things that I wouldn't be needing now that I was going to be a 'man' and all that. I was going to put all that stuff into black bags and carry it all down to Evington Road and dump it at one of the charity shops. Jas offered to drive me but I refused, saying that I needed the air and that I was a bit nervous about the wedding and wanted to get my head straight. Because I had agreed to the wedding, I was like a freeman of the city as far as my family were concerned. No more questions about where I was going and what I was doing. No more suspicions. All of which suited my plan.

I made four trips in all, packing into the bags all the things that I couldn't do without. The heaviest one contained my books and stuff, so I took it first. It was a long walk to Ady's place with a heavy black bag in each hand, and by midafternoon my arms were aching, but at least I now had the majority of my things out of the house. I used the clothes and other bits that I was leaving behind to disguise the fact that I had moved out in all but body: a pair of old jeans over a chair, a few CD cases on the bed, some magazines and so on. No-one asked me a thing as I moved my

---

3 **fake** [feɪk] false – 28 **suspicions** [səˈspɪʃənz] mistrust, wariness

stuff. I mean, I passed by my old man, my mum, Harry, both my sisters-in-law, uncles, aunts, you name it. It was like I was invisible to them as they went about the preparations for my wedding.

After I had returned from my last trip to Ady's, I shut myself in my room and chilled out, looking forward to the party later that evening, not because I was happy or excited about the wedding, but because I was nervous and excited about my new future, the one that I had in my head. I kept on turning it over and over in my mind until my brain started to ache and I needed to be able to forget about it. The party would be the perfect way to do that, with all the free booze everywhere and no-one bothered about whether I was pissed or not. They would probably encourage it, my family, because they saw hard drinking as a way of proving that you had become a man. To my brothers it showed that I had become 'one of them', and for my own purposes I needed to let them believe that for the next two days.

That evening I had to go through a ceremony where this yellow dough shit is slapped all over your face. It's called a *saggan*, which means 'blessing', and the dough is made up of flour, turmeric powder to give it colour and mustard oil. I'd seen it done to my brothers and thought that it was nasty then, but actually having the stuff slapped all over my face and neck by Jas and Baljit and all my aunts was like a nightmare. There I was, surrounded by all these cackling hags, all trying to coat me in this foul-smelling stuff that took about twenty minutes to wash off and I couldn't do anything about it. They did it out in the garden too, and because it was the end of November, it was quite cold.

Later on my family had gathered for the first of the pre-wedding parties. Some party it was going to be, not that I'd expected it to be much in the first place. All family parties went the same way. The men got together in one room, getting drunk, while the women congregated in another, gossiping and watching old wedding videos. There were some kids on the stairs – the sons and daughters of various first and second

---

25 **to cackle** to talk in a very loud and annoying way *(schnattern, gackern)* – 25 **hag** *(vul)* old woman, old witch – 34 **to congregate** to gather in a group

cousins, half of whose names I wasn't too sure of – and as I tried to get past them and up the stairs, I heard Ranjit call out after me from the front room.

'Oi! Wedding boy. Where you goin'? Come and have a beer, innit.'

'In a minute,' I replied, 'I'm just going to eat my dinner.'

'What you got there? Samosas?'

'No, just a cheese sandwich.'

'Cheese? Why you wanna eat cheese for? We got tandoori chicken coming in a minute an' you eating cheese. Come and have some of the real food, innit.'

'In a minute.'

'Then you coming to the pub with us, Manjit. Just us young 'uns. None of the fogeys.'

'Nah, I'll pass, man. I'll come down tomorrow. I'm a bit tired tonight.' There was no way I was going down the pub with them – act or no act. Instead I took a walk up to Ady's to finalize the plans for my cheat.

Chapter Thirty-two
Saturday 29th November

I woke up on the Saturday morning with a hangover, wondering why there was so much noise being made all over the house. I looked at my alarm clock and saw that it was only just past eight in the morning. Outside my bedroom door I could hear kids running about, one or more of them banging on my door every five minutes or so. The only one I recognized by sound was Ranjit's brat, Gurpal, who was screaming at the top of his voice, trying to sing some new bhangra tune, only he couldn't remember all the words.

As I lay in bed, my head aching from drinking a whole bottle of Bacardi with Ady the night before, I wondered how things were going to turn out for my nephew. At nearly five years of age, he was already well behind most kids of his age in his grasp of English. Everyone in the house apart from me spoke to him only in Punjabi and encouraged him to do the same. No-one ever read books to him, not even Jas, his mum, who had actually had a good education, something that I had once confused

---

14 **fogey** ['fəʊgi] old, strange guy – 25 – 31 **brat** little monster (negative word for "small child")

with having an intellect. In her case they really weren't the same thing. After all, it's not like she had used her education to her advantage. She seemed happy to play the quiet little Punjabi wife, always in the kitchen or looking after the kids. And she never complained either. Most of the time she tried to justify it, spouting the same rubbish about Punjabi values as my old man or my brothers. No doubt she'd have a couple more kids soon. Gurpal was like a lost cause already, although I had a feeling that by the time he reached my age, things would have changed so much that he'd probably rebel too.

I got out of bed and drew back the curtains. Outside it was sunny and bright, although there was a heavy frost on the ground. I opened my window and got a blast of chilly air which made me reach for a T-shirt. I found my fags in my jacket pocket and lit one, blowing the smoke out of the window, letting the ash fall on to the flat roof of the kitchen extension. There were a few people in the garden but they couldn't see me because they were too close to the kitchen door to see above the extension itself. Not that I really cared anymore. It was far too late in the game to worry about things like that. After I finished my fag, I pulled on my jeans and headed for the bathroom, hoping that it was free. From downstairs came the sound of women gossiping and a bhangra tape was playing in the living room. It was the start of another long day, I thought to myself as I shut the bathroom door, just before Gurpal managed to sneak in behind me.

By midday I was sitting in the front room drinking tea and wishing that I had my own television. The football was about to start and I wanted to watch it but the TV was in the living room and all the women had taken it over. I was desperate to see what was happening with Liverpool after another shit start to the season. For some strange reason, I was convinced that my own problems were mirrored by the problems faced by my football team. I know it sounds stupid but it was like I was waiting for Liverpool to have a wicked season because I was convinced that would see my own life pick up too. I was sitting on the old man's green velvet sofa, thinking about what I'd do if I was the Liverpool manager when my old man walked in, all bleary-eyed from a night of hard drinking.

'Manjit, beteh,' he said with his croak, his morning voice, 'Come, let's have a drink to celebrate your good luck.'

---

6 **to spout** *(inf)* to speak pompously

I looked up at him and fought back the urge to shake my head at the state that he was in, not to mention the fact that he wanted another drink so early in the morning. Instead I smiled at him and said no, answering him in Punjabi. 'Not yet, Daddy-ji. Later. I have to go into town to pick up my suit.'

'Haven't you bought it yet? I thought you got it when I gave you that money?'

'No, I ordered it,' I lied. I *was* actually going to buy a suit, but it would be a cheap one because I wanted to use as much of my cash windfall as I could for a deposit on my own flat.

'When are you going?'

'About an hour from now.'

'Do you need some more money?' asked my old man, swaying as if he had been caught in a strong wind, and belching. I wanted to say that I did but for some reason it came out as 'no'. The old man just shook his head and smiled. 'Now that you are one of us again, beteh, anything you want you can have. How much?'

'No, no. Honest. I don't need any more money.'

'Don't be an idiot, Manjit. Am I doing all of this for me? It's all for you. It's your life.'

Well, as soon as he said that, something inside me just snapped. I was seething. What did he mean that it was my life? None of this shit was my life. None of it was down to me. I had never asked him to arrange a wedding for me. I had never asked him to try and lumber me with some wife that I didn't want so that he could repay some old mate of his for a past favour. Sack that. I worked hard at keeping calm on the outside but my face must have gone a little red. It must have done so because there was a volcano erupting inside me – blood like lava. The old man didn't even notice, probably because he was still pissed from the night before, and he pulled out another roll of notes from his front pocket, more money than I had ever seen before. He counted out about a grand and put it on the table in front of me.

'There, have that,' he said, smiling and putting the rest back in his pocket.

'No, it's too much,' I said.

'Take it, Manjit. I won't ask you again,' he said. 'Anything that you don't use, you can put into your bank account. A married man needs to have money.'

---

10 **cash windfall** extra, unexpected money – 22 **to snap** *(here)* to break suddenly – 22 **to seethe** [siːð] *(here)* to be very angry – 25 **to lumber** to load, to burden

I nodded and looked at the grand in front of me. Damn right I was gonna put it into my bank account, but not for my life as a married man. For my new life, as a free man. I said a thank you, but as I got up to take my mug into the kitchen, the old man grabbed me and gave me a hug that nearly knocked the wind out of me.

'You see, Manjit,' he said, his breath reeking of stale booze. 'You are one of us. Ours. I know things have been wrong between us, I know. But haven't I made you a real man? Haven't I?'

I tried to break his hold but he was too strong and he just squeezed me for ages, tears in his eyes. I tried to look away from him but I couldn't. There were tears in my eyes too. Not because I felt sad or guilty. Not because I thought that he was right, or forgave him for anything that he had ever done to me. The fists in the face. The kicks in the back. The bruises on my legs that he'd put there with the old hockey stick he kept in the closet under the stairs – bruises that I'd explain away as football injuries to everyone except Ady. My tears were a sign that I was never going to be the man that he had tried to beat me into being. Never. And I knew, after that point, that I was never coming back. Any link that I had with my father was gone for good.

After I had to sit through another *saggan* that evening, I walked down Evington Drive to St Philip's church which sat at the end of Evington Road. My old man had hired the church hall for a party for all the men in my family – another Punjabi custom that meant that the women got to have the house to themselves to have their own party. The party at the hall was just an excuse for another piss-up, with loud bhangra music blasting out and panfuls of tandoori chicken and lamb curry being dished up. By the time I got there it was just past ten o'clock and most of the guests had already been there for a couple of hours. It was packed. I could see Harry and all his mates sitting next to where a bhangra DJ hired for the night had set up a table for his decks and stuff. Around the room I saw various uncles and cousins and second cousins, all throwing booze and meat down their throats like they'd never seen it before. My old man was staggering around the hall, shaking hands with people and topping up their glasses. He was hammered and I really didn't

7 **to reek** to stink

feel like talking to him so I looked around for a place to sit and have a bottle of Pils, which was the only beer that my old man had bought. The rest of the booze was either Bacardi or Famous Grouse, typical for most Punjabi wedding piss-ups.

I went and sat on my own, near the back of the hall, just watching as everyone around me got drunker and drunker, ignoring me even though I suppose I was the guest of honour as the one who was meant to be getting married. Ranjit and a couple of his mates finally noticed that I had turned up and came over with a plate of chicken and a bottle of Bacardi.

'It's wedding boy,' laughed Ranjit as I looked up at him and his mates.

'Awright?'

'Man, why you so late? It's your party.'

'Don't feel like it,' I replied, taking a swig from my warm bottle of Pils. One of Ranjit's mates, a six-foot-bloke called Surjit who was so fat that he probably hadn't seen his own knob for about five years without the aid of a mirror, ruffled my hair and then laughed.

'Don't worry, you little shit. After tomorrow it'll be your party every night, innit.' They all started laughing at his stupid joke. Ranjit poured Bacardi into a glass on the table next to me and pushed it my way.

'Here, drink a man's drink, not that water you got there. You're a Jat Punjabi – not a bloody Hindu.'

They broke into laughter again, like a pack of hyenas, giggling at their own ignorance. I blanked them and the glass of Bacardi, taking another swig of my beer.

'And if you need some tips. About how to do it, innit. Just ask. We all experts, man,' said Surjit, winking at me. I was really tempted to make a crack at him but decided to keep quiet.

'Soon you'll be out and about with us guys, innit. No more hanging about with that monkey and all them *goreh*,' said another of Ranjit's mates, a skinny, greasy-haired bloke called Dev in a pair of shiny grey trousers.

I glared at him for about ten seconds before I flipped. I mean there's some things that you can keep quiet at and that, but what he'd just said made me want to kill him. I stood and faced up to him, even though he was about two inches taller than me.

'You wanna say that again, Dev?'

---

17 **knob** [nɒb] (*BE inf*) penis – 26 **hyena** [haɪˈiːnə] African carnivorous animal that makes a sound like wild laughter

Ranjit looked at me and then at his mate and smiled. I waited for Dev to say something but he just stood there, smirking.

'Well? You wanna call my best mate a monkey again?'

'Chill out, Manjit,' said Ranjit, putting his hand on my shoulder.

I shrugged it off and stood my ground. 'No. Tell your friend here to keep his racist gob shut or I'm going to fill it with my bottle.'

Ranjit stood and looked at me for a minute and then burst into laughter. One by one his mates followed suit, all except Dev who just looked away. Surjit came and put his arm around my shoulders and picked up the glass of Bacardi that Ranjit had poured for me. He drank it down in one go and then let out a grunt. I pushed him off and turned to face Ranjit, who was still smiling, like something really funny had just happened.

'You know, Manjit, I always thought that you were a bit of a poof, innit. But today you showed us you got the fight in you, like a real Jat man.'

I shook my head at him and decided to go outside for some air. But before leaving I said something that I had wanted to say for ages.

'I ain't nothing like you and your mates, and I never will be, no matter what happens. And you can tell Dev that I'll catch him out on the street one day. See how tough he feels then.'

Outside Ekbal was smoking a spliff with some other lads, all distant relations. I found them hiding around the side of the hall behind some tall bushes. 'Nah, man,' he said to me, 'I can't believe you are going through with this shit. I thought you didn't want it?'

'I don't want to do it, man,' I replied, 'I just ain't got a choice.'

'Sack that, Manny, you don't have to do nuttin', man.'

'I can't just not do it,' I lied, not wanting to let my cheat out of the bag. 'What am I gonna do? I'd have to leave home and everything. My family would cut me off.'

'Let 'em. I don't care about shit like that. Man's gotta do what he wants to, otherwise why bother at all. Ain't no-one runnin' my life for me.'

'We'll see, Ekky. Not that you'll ever be in my position. Your family's different.'

I handed back the spliff and walked back into the hall, Ekky's words floating around in my head as I tried to avoid Ranjit, his mates and Harry's little gang. I don't know what time I eventually left for the short walk back to the house but somewhere along the way I had to stop and throw up, the combination of beer and nerves overcoming my attempts to keep control of my stomach. I think Harry and one of his mates were behind me as I was throwing up, only I can't remember. All I can recall is thinking, This is it. This is IT! It was finally time to type my cheat onto the screen and let the game commence, with all the best weapons, for once, on *my* side.

Chapter Thirty-three
Sunday 30th November

I got woken up at half past five on the morning of my seventeenth birthday. My wedding day. After fighting my way into the bathroom and getting ready, I headed downstairs and made some coffee which I took into the living room where one of my uncles, Pritam, was sorting out a box of red carnations for all the men to wear in their lapels.

'Good morning, mate,' he said as I sat down on the sofa, next to some cousin or other.

'Awright, Uncle-ji. How's things?'

'Things OK, mate, you know. Taxi business going well.'

'Sorted.'

'Bit like you, mate. We all thought you were gonna turn out a wrong one, you know, with all that pissing about you done. But you turn out OK. Good luck for the wedding, Manjit.'

We were due to leave for Derby around nine that morning, with the majority of the guests following in a specially hired coach or two, the *janeth* it's called. Punjabi weddings are all about ancient traditions that have been handed down for a few centuries. One of those traditions says that the boy and his family must go to the place where the girl lives, in this case Derby, marry her and then bring her back to his family home. There are all these notions of honour and stuff and in a way I suppose it's quite romantic, if you like that kind of thing – you know, the groom bringing his new bride back on his horse, or in my case in the back of a maroon Mercedes that Ranjit had borrowed from one of his friends for the wedding. A turban was

---

14 **carnation** strong-smelling garden flower (usually red, pink, or white) *(Nelke)* –
15 **lapel** [lə'pel] outward fold of cloth on a jacket or coat from the shoulder down over the chest – 20 **sorted** *(BE inf)* properly arranged, provided with everything necessary – 31 **notion** idea – 34 **maroon** dark brownish red

tied to my head and a piece of cloth called a *phullah* attached to my shoulders; my sisters and cousin sisters held this as I made my way out to the car, having been given a piece of Indian sweetmeat as a blessing. The car looked really tacky. Gold and white ribbons were attached to the front of it and a huge gold coloured *khanda* – the symbol of Sikhism – was on the back shelf. Written across the rear windscreen were the words '*Raj Karegah Khalsa*' (which meant 'the Sikh brotherhood will reign') and, embarrassingly, the words 'Punjab Express'. The Sikh symbols were purely for show – not one member of my family was actually a Sikh in anything but name – but the 'Punjab Express' bit was the kind of thing Harry loved.

My mum and some of her cronies stood in the doorway and poured saffron oil onto the step just before I left. My old dear had tears in her eyes and kept on praising God. I wanted to say goodbye to her because I really was leaving but my sisters-in-law got in the way and lots of other people crowded around me, including Ranjit and my cousin Ekbal who just shook his head and laughed when he saw me in my turban.

'Man, you look like Gunga Din in that,' he said as I got into the back of the car next to him. Ranjit, who was driving, got in the front and then Harry waddled up, his suit looking like it was going to burst under the pressure of keeping all that fat in check, and climbed into the front passenger side.

'Ready to lose your virginity then, you poof?' he said smiling and exposing his yellow teeth.

I ignored him and closed my eyes, trying to clear my thoughts, my mind filled with last-minute nerves and doubts. I knew what I had to do, had it all planned, but even at this stage I was feeling unsure. And then I saw the picture of Jag's kid, Mia, in my mind and I perked up, remembering everything that he had said to me about doing my own thing, and that I wasn't being selfish. Harry made a few more cracks before Ekbal called him a fat bastard and then Ranjit told us to shut up as he pulled off.

We were just getting on to the motorway when I told Ranjit that I needed to go to the loo. He sighed, telling me that I should have gone back at the house, but I reminded him that it was my wedding day and he had to listen to me for a change. Harry started sniggering and said that I was shitting myself because I wasn't a real man.

4 **sweetmeat** (*BE old-fashioned*) sweet – 4 – 13 **crony/cronies** negative word fpr friends – 20 **Gunga Din** 1892 poem by Rudyard Kipling, telling of a waterboy in the British colonial army (here it is negatively used for people from Asia) – 31 **to perk up** to become cheerful, active and interested – 39 **to snigger** to laugh in an unkind and mocking way (*kichern*)

'He's just scared, innit, 'case his missus is too much woman for him.'

'Your missus must be too much for you – and at least I don't fire blanks,' I said, making Ekbal and Ranjit laugh.

'Better watch your mouth, you little shit. Don't want a black eye on your wedding day, do you?'

'Listen, fat boy, after all the bruises you lot have given me since I was a kid, I can take it. One of these days, Harry, I'm gonna get my own back. I got you and all your mates in check.'

'What you think...?'

'Shut it, both of you. I'm the eldest one here, innit. You got to listen to me,' said Ranjit, pulling into Leicester Forest East services. 'Here, go to the bog if you have to, but you better hurry. If we're late, Daddy-ji will look bad in front of all the guests.'

He pulled into the car park and parked up. I got out and headed for the toilets, ducking into the first cubicle inside, wondering if anyone had noticed me in my Gunga Din outfit. Someone had written the words 'WOOHAH' on the door in red ink. In the next cubicle someone coughed – two short sounds, almost like a code.

We got to Derby about half ten and headed for the Sikh temple near the old Derby county football ground, the Baseball Ground. The area, which had a big black and Asian population, was a bit run-down but the temple was brand new and stood out amongst the dirty brown brick buildings because it was white with a gold dome top. Once Ranjit had parked up, behind the coach that had brought the rest of the *janeth*, my old man came up and asked why we had taken so long. Ranjit told him that we had stopped for me to go to the loo and that I had been in there for a good fifteen minutes which was only a slight exaggeration. My old man swore in Punjabi and then told us to come over to where everyone else was waiting. As I got out of the car, holding my *phullah*, Ekbal tried to straighten my jacket.

'Man, I told you to take it off in the car. It's all gathered up on your shoulders and back,' he said.

'Leave it, Ekky, it's cool. It's gonna get even more creases in it by the time I'm finished,' I replied, following my brothers over to where my family stood facing the girl's family, with a twenty-metre channel between them, like some gang war face-off.

---

1 **'case his missus** (*spoken*) "in case his wife..." – 4 **to fire blanks** (literally): a cartridge filled with powder but without a bullet (*Platzpatrone*), here: "to ejaculate semen which will not make his wife pregnant" (he is insulting his brother's virility) – 13 **bog** (*BE, inf*) toilet

I had to stand through about three different ceremonies that involved the giving of gold rings and blankets and things, from her family to mine – something called a *milni*, or meeting. This was another tradition I hated – the fact that the girl's side had to give the boy's family so much stuff. I stood through it all yawning my head off and waiting for a chance to grab some time by myself.

The thing was, after that point no-one left me alone for a minute. If it wasn't my sisters-in-law fussing over me, it was my old man – already well pissed – telling me to remember the order of the ceremony, and asking me if I needed this or that, mainly money again. And different aunti-jis and uncle-jis were coming over to tell me what a good boy I was and how they were so glad that I had straightened myself out while I was in India.

Then I saw Parmjit – the cousin who had been left in India for a whole year – standing in a corner of the car park, two kids in tow. A young woman in a Punjabi suit approached him, said something and then shouted at him. As she turned and walked off I realized that it was his wife. He watched her go and then smiled over at me, feebly. I hadn't seen him for a few years and he had put on loads of weight, just like Harry and Ranjit had after they got married. But the worst thing about his appearance was the fact that his hair had begun to recede and he had these huge dark circles under his eyes, bags big enough to carry shopping home in. How old was he? Twenty-one? Twenty-two? I turned to my old man who was now standing next to me like a farmer with his prize-winning bull, all grins and handshakes for the blokes that filed past heading for the tea and samosas that were being served inside.

'I need to go to the toilet again,' I told him, looking at my watch. Eleven o'clock. It was time.

'What is the matter with you. Are you possessed or something?' he replied, in Punjabi.

'I'll be quick.' I spoke in English which wound him up.

'What are you? A *gorah*? Talk in Punjabi. No-one wants your English here. This is a Punjabi temple.'

'Yeah, yeah.' I looked at my watch again, starting to feel the first signs of panic.

'You have to come and have some tea first with the rest of us.'

'You go in. I'm only going to be a couple of minutes.'

---

20 **feeble** ['fiːbəl] weak – 23 **to recede** to go back, go away – 32 **to be possessed** to be controlled by a dark force

This time I spoke in Punjabi and he relented, telling me to hurry up. I walked into the temple and asked one of the attendants where the toilets were. He told me that there were two sets, one on the first floor near the front, and another set on the ground floor around the back. I headed for those, sweat beginning to form on my forehead even though it was a cold day. I walked through an empty hall area and out through a set of doors, down a long corridor and into what looked like a half-finished kitchen area.

At the far end from where I stood, right at the back of the building were two fire exits, one in each corner. The way out! I headed for them, pulling off my turban and *phullah*.

The first exit wouldn't budge. Panicking a bit, I ran over to the other one and tried that. It wouldn't open either and I started to feel paranoid. I mean, if they didn't open, my only escape would be through the front of the temple and I'd definitely get spotted then. It was enough of a risk going out the back way as someone would almost certainly see me, but it was less likely to be a member of my family. I barged the exit again, really hammering into it, and it gave a little but still wouldn't open. I stood and thought for a moment and then I started to think about how far I'd come and how much I had taken, all the shit and the beatings and the verbal stuff. All the lies my family had told me. All the racist stuff they had fed me about blacks and whites and anyone who wasn't a Jat Punjabi. My head just exploded on the inside.

It was nearly ten past eleven. No time. I launched at the fire exit, using the sole of my right foot to kick it. I did it once, twice, three times. Then again. And again. And then BLAM! The door was open and I was free, running out of the temple on to a narrow back street. I had a quick look down the street but it was deserted. Where the hell was Ady?

As I ran I threw off my jacket and pulled my tie loose. The buttons on my shirt broke away and the first people I passed – an old couple out walking their dog – gave me a strange look as I pelted by, throwing my tie behind me. I ran down the road, side-stepping a young Asian kid in ragga gear whose eyes nearly popped out of his head in surprise as I rounded the bend in the road that led up towards a row of shops. As I ran I looked behind me and saw a white car pull out onto the main road, similar to the one that Harry's best mate drove. I couldn't believe it. They

---

1 **to relent** to give in – 13 **to budge** to move – 16 **to spot** to see – 19 **to barge** [bɑːdʒ] to push suddenly and in a rough way – 26 **to launch** [lɔːntʃ] to start on – 35 **to pelt** to run

couldn't be following me already. They couldn't have found out yet!

I took a left into a side street and sprinted to the end, my lungs about to burst. Right. Then right again and back down a parallel street. Back on myself. The car, a white, old-shaped Cavalier sped round the corner after me and passed me by before stopping in the road. The door on the driver's side came open and the sound of hip hop music blasted out. I stopped running and approached the car, realizing that it wasn't anyone from my family. Ady was behind the wheel, grinning at me.

'Your taxi, sir,' he said, laughing as soon as he'd spoken.

'Where the hell have you been?' I shouted, peeling off my shirt to expose a grey hooded top underneath. I got into the passenger seat, throwing my shirt out onto the road.

'Chill out, my yout'. I'm here, ain't I? Happy Birthday.'

As I pulled the door shut he drove off, wheel spinning down to the bottom of the road as Busta Rhymes kicked the ballistics.

'*Woo Hah!!! I got you all in check.*'

---

17 **Busta Rhymes** New York hip hop star with Jamaican roots – 17 **Busta Rhymes kicked the ballistics** the extremely loud sound of Busta Rhymes' rap music started up

now

Chapter Thirty-four
Tuesday 30th November

It's two years to the day since I did my disappearing act and I feel that maybe I should explain my actions. It's something that I've thought about for ages. Ever since that day in Derby. I don't regret anything that I did: the cheat, doing a runner and taking all that money. I still feel that it was something that my family owed to me after all the years of treating me like some kind of private possession and not as another human being.

I'm nineteen now and I live at Lisa's parents' house, in her room, only we're not together any more. She's taking a year off, just like she always said, and travelling around the Far East. She e-mails me twice a week and I still love her as much as I ever did, only in a different way. Her parents, Amanda and Ben, took me in after I left. I was going to get a flat but Ben told me to bank my money so that I could use it to pay college fees when I eventually returned to my education. They were a godsend and I love them both to bits although Ady tells them they are like those couples in Australian soap operas – the ones that take in all the waifs and strays.

I'm still working nights for the same supermarket, waiting to retake my GCSEs. I've been provisionally accepted for college but I can't start until next September which is fine with me. I want to save up as much money as possible to add to what is left in my bank account – Ady helped me spend some – and I should be able to get some sort of funding. It's something that I need to find out about. I might have to go to night school to do my A levels and work during the day. Whatever. The thing is, all the choices that I make now are about me. The person that I want to be. Not the person that my old man tried to beat and pressure me into being. And that makes everything that I did worthwhile.

I haven't spoken to anyone in my immediate family since my wedding day that wasn't. From time to time I'll see Harry or Ranjit and Jas, walking through town or driving by but if they see me, they don't show it. I was scared that they would come after me, find me and try to make me go back. Ekbal, who I see out and about all the time, told me that for the first few months after I left, that's exactly what they'd threatened to do. Harry had talked about beating the crap out of me, sending me to India for good, all that sort of stuff. Only I kept a real low profile for

18 **the waifs and strays** [weɪfsənd'streɪz] homeless children

about a year afterwards. I'd try not to go out in the day and totally avoided going anywhere near Evington Road. If I did go into town or whatever, I'd be looking around every two minutes, watching my back like some IRA supergrass. I didn't enjoy doing it but I had no choice. There was no way I was ever going back to that way of life. No way.

In the end, I didn't have to leave. My family moved to Oadby where they bought two houses next door to each other so that they could carry on playing happy extended families. Jas and Ranjit have a little girl now too, but Harry still hasn't managed to prove his manhood. Ekbal told me that I stopped being a factor in their lives after they had moved. No-one spoke about me, or even mentioned my name. It was like I had never existed at all. Apparently my old man wasn't badly hurt by what I did; he just kept on drinking and working and visiting the gurudwara on Sundays. And my mother, despite all her threats and her drama queen hysterics, never killed herself or died of shock or anything like that. Their lives just went on like before, only they didn't have me to ignore or beat up or anything. My father only had two sons now.

I still have this idea that one day I might be accepted back into the fold, like they did with Jag, but I know deep down inside that it won't happen. They haven't even spoken to Jag since he helped me to escape from India. I call him up every other week though. Or I send him e-mails on my new computer. He's cool, Jag, still the same, although he hasn't managed to make it over to England yet. That's changing though. He's coming over to London soon and I'm going to go and stay with him and his family, who I can't wait to meet.

The only thing that I regret about the whole cheat thing is the fact that I left it until my wedding day to carry it out. At the time it felt like the right thing to do, the best way to take my revenge. I was angry and hurt and all those things, so much so that I wasn't thinking with a clear head. I confused all the hate that I felt for my family and their stupid traditions with being a Sikh or being a Punjabi. It was all one big whole to me, maybe because I was too young to see the difference.

OK, so I got my revenge on my old man and my stupid brothers and that, but I also disrespected the girl's family and it wasn't their fault at all. And I disrespected the temple and the

---

4 **supergrass** a criminal who gives the police information about other criminals
– 22 **the fold** *(here)* family, community

Sikh religion and I never meant to do that. Not that I'm a Sikh myself or anything. I'm still trying to work out whether there actually is a God at all. But I did confuse being a Jat Punjabi in the way that my old man saw it, with being a Sikh, which is something totally different.

I've been reading up on it lately and I've found that Sikhism preaches tolerance and equality towards everyone, a bit like an Asian version of Christianity, only without the Adam and Eve bit. Men, women. Black, white. All the same. The problem is that people like my old man tie in all these old traditions to the religion – arranged marriages, all that racist shit, the caste system stuff, things which are nothing to do with religion and more to do with culture and politics and social norms.

My old man and his mates are the ones who are really confused; they're too ignorant to change their ways or even realize that they don't know what they are on about. They don't even understand the religion that they try to brainwash their own kids with. They just piss about with it until it suits their needs, fits their own way of thinking, and that, as far as I'm concerned, is wrong. Just as I was wrong for allowing myself to confuse everything and put it all together in one big whole, until anything and everything that was Punjabi or Sikh became part of the problem.

As for Ady, well he's the same old nutter he always was. He's still living at his brother's with Sarah and Zac, and working with me. Sarah is studying to become a nurse and Zac just gets to be more and more like his dad everyday. They can't take him to the supermarket without him toddling off after the girls – Ady has even taught him to say 'honeyz' in the same stupid accent he always put on. It's been interesting to see Ady grow up since Zac came along and he seems to have coped well, even when he had to be up all night changing nappies. Back when we were kids the man couldn't get out of bed most mornings. But then again Sarah keeps him on his toes.

I owe Ady a lot. Without him the cheat wouldn't have worked. The way he planted those extra clothes in that toilet cubicle at Leicester Forest East, borrowing his brother's car even though he hasn't got a licence. All that stuff. And to top it all, he named me as Zac's godfather. It was a little later than normal, granted

---

24 **nutter** [ˈnʌtə] *(inf)* crazy person – 32 **nappy** *(BE)* diaper *(AE)* a piece of thick cloth fastened round a baby's bottom *(Windel)* – 39 **godfather** a man who agrees to take responsibility for a child's (religious) upbringing *(Pate)*

– Zac was six months old when Ady asked me – but I was thrilled to bits.

And then there's me. Dreaming about travelling and writing and all that other stuff, and still waiting for Liverpool to win the Premiership. My life isn't exactly like a garden of roses at the moment. I have to work hard, stacking shelves all night long, and sometimes I have to watch every single penny that I spend. But my life is mine and that's what I've always wanted. And I've got a new girlfriend too, a girl who works part-time on the reception desk at the supermarket. She's called Jenny and she's great, dark brown hair and bright blue eyes, and she's really intelligent too. We're into a lot of the same things, like books and music and stuff, and even though she's not Lisa, she's still wicked. She's actually coming round in a minute to help me celebrate my birthday. We're going out with Ady and Sarah. It should be a laugh. But whatever it is, I'm doing it because I choose to do it.

And that is what all this stuff has been about.

the end

5 **Premiership** the top professional soccer championship in England

Additional texts

Immigration from India, Pakistan and Bangladesh

Date

1947	The British divide the Indian sub-continent into the countries of India, West Pakistan and East Pakistan. Up to two million people die in violence between religious groups (mainly Hindus, Muslims and Sikhs). Many people want to flee the trouble.
1948	British Nationality Act. The concept of a *citizen of the United Kingdom and Colonies* (CUKC) is born. There is very little difference between the rights of CUKCs and other British subjects, all of whom had the right at any time to enter the United Kingdom and live there.
1955	By 1955, there are 11,000 Indian and Pakistani people in Britain. Between 1955 and 1962, over 250,000 people arrive from all over the Commonwealth.
1950s and 60s	Several hundred thousand people from India and Pakistan enter Britain in search of a better material life. They can earn up to 30 times more than at home. Many come from Northern India and Pakistan.
early 1960s	Construction of the Mangla Dam, Pakistan. This destroys around 250 villages, leaving 100,000 people homeless; many of these move to Britain.
1962	The Commonwealth Immigrants Act means that Commonwealth Citizens no longer have the automatic right to move to Britain. People rush to Britain before the new law makes it too difficult (1961: about 66,000 people).
1971	East Pakistan gains independence in a bloody war and becomes Bangladesh. Many refugees enter the UK. The Immigration Act in the UK effectively stops primary immigration (people coming to work and settle). Only relatives of those already settled in UK may now enter.
1972	28,000 Asian people who have been expelled from Uganda (Africa) by the dictator Idi Amin come to Britain. Many settle in Leicester.
1981	The Conservative government passes the new Nationality Act, removing the right to British citizenship from many people from "new Commonwealth" nations (including those from the Indian subcontinent).
2007	There are now between one and two million British Muslims (2% - 4% of the population), over half of them born in Britain.

Statistics on the Ethnicity of Leicester and the UK

This chart (Figure 1) shows the ethnic backgrounds which the people of Leicester assigned to themselves in the 2001 census.

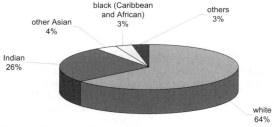

Figure 1: Leicester: Ethnicity

Compare this to the ethnic composition for the whole of England and Wales (Figure 2). Leicester has proportionally one of the highest coloured populations in the UK, and the largest Indian populations of any local authority area in England and Wales. It has been predicted that Leicester will be one of the first local authorities in which white people will form a minority of the population.

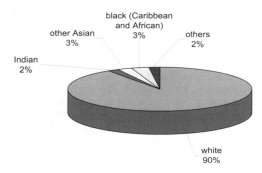

Figure 2: England and Wales: Ethnicity

Compared with the national average (Figure 4), Leicester has a high proportion of Sikhs. Like Manjit's family, nearly all of these 12,000 or so people (2001 census) have their roots in the Punjab in Northern India / Eastern Pakistan. However, proportionately speaking, there are even larger Sikh populations to the west of London. Ealing and Hounslow each have Sikh populations of over 8%, Slough can boast of being 9% Sikh.

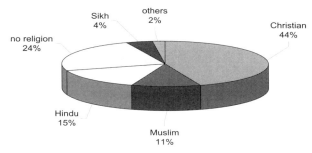

Figure 3: Religions: Leicester

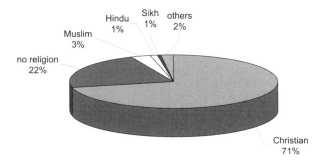

Figure 4: Religions: England and Wales

Map of Great Britain, the Midlands, Leicester and Derby

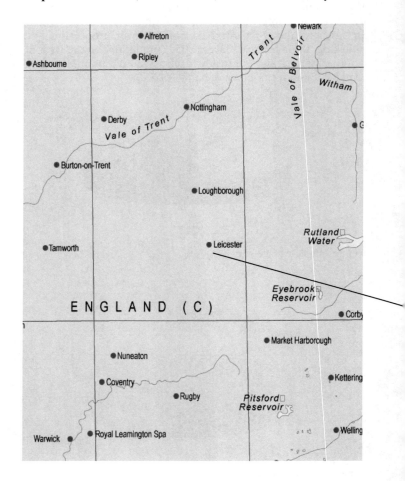

180

Map of India and the Punjab